Northopraxis
or
From Pastoral Life

By

Fr. Bohdan Hladio

HDM Press, Inc
2009

Northopraxis
or
From Pastoral Life
HDM Press, Inc./2009
P.O.Box 128
Rives Junction, MI 49277

Information may be obtained from:
HDM Press, Inc.
P.O.Box 128
Rives Junction, MI 49277

Library of Congress Control Number: 2008943622

ISBN: 9780964347861

Printed in the United States of America
by Sheridan Books, Chelsea, Michigan.

Table of Contents

Moral Issues

ACKNOWLEDGMENT

Fr. Ihor Kutash, the editor of the Visnyk/Herald (the newspaper of the Ukrainian Orthodox Church of Canada), called me in the autumn of 1997 to ask whether I would consider writing a monthly column for the paper. With the blessing of Metropolitan Wasyly of blessed memory I agreed. The book you hold in your hands is a direct result of Fr. Ihor's request.

With God's help these columns have been appearing monthly for 11 years now. In the meantime, while serving as parish priest at St. Vladimir's Sobor in Hamilton, Ontario, I was blessed to apply, and be accepted as a member of the Community Editorial Board of the Hamilton Spectator, giving me opportunity to write for the general public in a large, daily newspaper as well.

Through the years I found that many people were edified by these columns, and more than once some suggested that they should be edited and published in book form. Given my pastoral and administrative responsibilities for many years I felt that such a thing was simply impossible. At the urging, and especially due to the prayers and blessing of Mother Gabriella, Fr. Roman Braga, and all the mothers and sisters of the Holy Dormition Monastery in Rives Junction, Michigan, this suggestion somehow became a reality.

I wish to thank all those who have contributed in any way to the publication of this volume: the parishioners I have had the honour to serve at St. Vladimir's Sobor in Hamilton, the Vancouver Island Parish District, Holy Cross Mission in Winnipeg and here at St. John the Baptist Church in Oshawa, Ontario; my brother priests who have been very supportive and helpful with their suggestions and advice, especially Frs. Andrew Jarmus and Gene Maximiuk; and all the Orthodox clergy and laity from every Orthodox jurisdiction who have taught me much about the breadth of beauty within and among all our various "small 't'" traditions.

A special note of thanks must be extended to my family: first and foremost my wife Tania to whom this book is dedicated. A priest could not hope to have a better wife and help-mate. My children Andre, Nina and Yuri also deserve thanks. It is my greatest joy that they are all "of the Church," and all of them have been, each in their own way, extremely helpful to me in my priestly ministry. My parents, brothers, and sisters also deserve a note of gratitude for all they have taught me about Christ-like love.

It is my most heart-felt prayer that the articles included in this collection will inform and edify the reader. For everything in this book that is good, true and beneficial thank God. For that which is not, forgive me and pray for me.

Fr. Bohdan Hladio
St. Patapius of Thebes

Note: *All articles appearing in this collection were first published in the Visnyk/Herald, the official organ of the Ukrainian Orthodox Church of Canada, with the exception of "Limits and Expectations" and "Homosexuality and Marriage" which were first published in the Hamilton Spectator. The kind permission of Ecclesia Publishing and the Hamilton Spectator to republish these articles in book form is gratefully acknowledged.*

INTRODUCTION

When the author wrote this book he quite likely did not realize that he was preparing a very good manual of pastoral practice for priests just arriving from Europe.

Orthodoxy in the United States and Canada does not resemble Orthodoxy in Eastern Europe or in the Balkans region. It possesses the same dogma, the same mysteries and is the same universal Church; but the character, administration and mentality of the faithful is different. The content of this book leads the reader to immediately understand the pulse of the spiritual life of Orthodox Christians on this continent.

Fr. Bohdan Hladio, born in Pennsylvania, in his priestly life has served in all administrative positions open to a lay priest—from administrator of a small parish to the chancellor of a metropolia. His intention was to put in writing, in a descriptive way, his personal experiences, the situations he encountered, the drama of situations many times impossible to resolve, even the frustrations and disappointments encountered by an honest and dedicated priest in his pastoral activity here in America.

A personal feeling of sadness emanates from much of the book, because most of the time things are not the way they should be. This suggests realities which must be considered when talking about the Orthodox Church in the United States and Canada.

Orthodoxy was brought to the new continent by the immigrants of various countries of Eastern Europe and it is maintained through the newcomers who fight tenaciously that the churches in America remain ethnic ghettos. Because of the exaggerated chauvinistic attitude of the newcomers and of the hierarchy, Orthodoxy has not become yet a reality of this country where we live, in other words, an Autocephalus Church with a synod of bishops and a primate.

A priest newly arrived in America will be surprised to find out that his parish does not resemble a church, but more a national club under tension; the struggle between the old generations already integrated in the local culture and the new immigrants who resist any kind of change. Not to mention the desperate situation of the converts who would like to be Orthodox without having to belong to an ethnic group.

National identity, language and ethnicity are temporary and as the OCA Metropolitan Jonah has said, after three or four generations in a foreign country they disappear. Orthodoxy however, is eternal, catholic and apostolic; it is neither Romanian, nor Russian, nor American. It is not the language nor the customs that save us, it is the Church. National-cultural propaganda is a political matter and it is the concern of the consular agents of the various Embassies, and not of the priests and bishops.

This being said, Fr. Bohdan's book suggests a new point of interest: Ethnic and cultural interests motivate the Orthodox faithful in America to ignore the mystical aspect of the Church as a Eucharistic center, where people unite with Christ and each other, thus forming the Mystical Body of Christ, with no consideration of ethnicity and nationality. It is a paradoxical situation; on one hand the newcomers resist assimilation by the ostentatious display of their national identity, and on the other hand they acquiesce to the negative influence of Protestants and Catholics, considering the Church more an institution rather than a place of salvation. You are not a member of the Church because you have been baptized, but because your name is on a list of members and you pay dues like in any other club or organization. The kitchen and the hall of the Church is a place for parties, cultural festivities, conferences, political rallies and fund raisers; more so, some have bars where you can buy alcoholic beverages.

It is therefore surprising for a priest who comes from an Orthodox country where there is a spiritual life, to find that he is controlled by the faithful that belong to the Parish Council or the General Assembly. In Eastern Europe Orthodoxy is hierarchal, not congregational. The priest is a spiritual father and not simply a payed employee who is told: "Father we pay you, you must do what we tell you." Even the religious activities, Sunday schools and Bible studies have a Protestant structure. It is not knowledge that saves us, but prayer and participation in the Holy Mysteries of the Church, because the Holy Spirit does not take into account knowledge, but the sanctity of life.

I consider Father Bohdan's book extremely important and I recommend it to all Orthodox faithful, as well as to priests. This book suggests ideas that force us to think about our situation as Orthodox Christians on this continent, where God has sent us not to make money, but to open the doors of Orthodoxy for those who are searching for it, but cannot find it because they run into the barriers of ethnicity. At the final judgement we will be asked to give an account for the faith which was entrusted to us—did we spread the Gospel of Christ, or were we an obstacle to the spreading of the Gospel? How will we respond?

Fr. Roman Braga
Hieromartyr Ignatios the God-bearer;
2008

PARISH LIFE

The Real Thing

"How do we increase the number of parishioners?" "How can we engage our inactive parishioners?" "How can we bring our youth back to the Church?" Such questions are heard in Orthodox parishes all over North America.

The Christian faith in our contemporary world is under attack from within and from without. The doctrines, moral teachings, and polity of the Church are regularly assailed in society, academia, and the media. Our young people are generally very uninformed about their faith, and virtually defenseless when antagonistically confronted about Christian beliefs and practices.

Add to this the "cult of the individual" as well as the atomization of society and we should not be surprised that it is sometimes difficult to find people willing to become members, let alone active members, of our parishes.

Is there anything we might do to actually strengthen and increase the numbers of our parishioners? Is there anything we might do to not only defend ourselves, but answer the criticisms leveled at us by the secular world, as well as those who, having disavowed much of the belief and practice of traditional Christianity, still call themselves "Christians?"

"Ours must be an Orthodoxy not only of doctrine, but of deed." These words point to an important truth. Perhaps the reason our parishes are not bursting with faithful has to do with the relationship between our doctrines and our deeds, or, as St. Paul puts it, between our truth and our love.

In his Epistle to the Ephesians, St. Paul writes: *". . . speaking the truth in love, we are to grow up in every way into Him who is the head, into Christ, from Whom the whole body, joined and knit together by every joint with which it is supplied, when each part is working properly, makes bodily growth and upholds itself in love"*

(Eph. 4:15-16). In other words, it is not enough to have the truth, to understand the truth, or to speak the truth—it is our calling first and foremost to live the truth.

The "growth of the body" which St. Paul mentions is the building up of the Church, which he claims is "upheld in love." So perhaps the reason we have problems within parishes, trouble evangelizing the heterodox, and fail to keep our children as members is a due to a defect in the quality of our love.

Parishioners often speak of how they wish new members would join the parish. When asked "why?" the response is often something like "so we can pay the bills," or "so we can continue to have services" or "so we do not have to close the doors." Such an attitude is not primarily concerned with what good the parish might do for the new member, but rather with what the newcomer can do for the parish. The love of such people is turned inward—to the parish, or community, or self—not outward, to the newcomer or stranger. It is about "we," not about "them." Most people, when approached in such a manner, instinctively feel a sense of discomfort and turn away.

When younger people are asked why they do not come to church a common response is "because I do not get anything out of the services." When older people are faced with change in parish life (e.g., the introduction of a liturgical language understandable to their grandchildren, a change in singing style, or even the participation of youth in the Liturgy) they often react negatively. "When we die, father, then you can do what you want!" or "This is the way we have done it for 50 years—why should we change now?" are common responses.

The attitudes of both the young and the old in the previous paragraph have one thing in common—they both assume that the Church exists to fulfill their own personal "spiritual needs" as they themselves define them.

Why does the Church really exist? To witness to the life, the ministry and the Gospel of Jesus Christ. To proclaim Christ's death and Resurrection. To teach the world what Life really is. To show the world what Love is.

It is said that our contemporary world is experiencing a crisis of love. Everyone, Christian and non-Christian, religious and atheistic, is in favor of love. Love is universally regarded as a virtue to be cultivated. But what is love? How do we define love? How does Christian love differ from the love of the Buddhist, the Atheist, or the Animist? *"You shall love the Lord your God with all your heart, with all your soul, and with all your mind. This is the first and greatest commandment. And the second is like it: you shall love your neighbor as yourself"* (Matt. 22:37-38).

Lesson number one: Christian love is not self-centered, but centered upon God and the neighbor. *"Love your enemies, do good to those who hate you, bless those who curse you and pray for those who spitefully use you"* (Luke 6:27:28).

Lesson number two: Christian love is unconditional, it is not confined to any particular group, but extended to everyone, always, and at all times—even those we do not like, even those who hate us. *"By this we know love, because He laid down His life for us. And we also ought to lay down our lives for the brethren. But whoever has this world's goods, and sees his brother in need, and shuts up his heart from him, how does the love of God abide in him? My little children, let us not love in word or in tongue, but in deed and in truth"* (1 John 3:16-18).

Lesson number three: Christian love must be active and sacrificial, love in "deed and truth," "laying down our lives" for others.

The Church exists so that her members might not only know God and worship Him, but that they might actually serve God by serving their fellow man. And this is precisely where our attempts at parish renewal tend to break down. We offer worship services, seminars, retreats and educational programs for personal spiritual growth, as well as cultural and social activities. But our parishes often lack a means whereby the parishioners might, in the name of Christ, serve the physical needs of the greater community.

The majority of our active parishioners are also active in their community. They work for charitable and service organizations, support acts of benevolence with monetary donations, and engage in personal acts of mercy towards the poor, the marginalized, the sick and the aged. They do this, no doubt, because of their faith. But most of this work is done outside the context of the parish. We should never do anything for show (cf. Matt. 6: 2-4), yet it is important that both parishioners as well as guests see that the parish community is openly engaged in following Jesus' teachings regarding acts of mercy. Our Lord tells us that we will be judged on the basis of how we treat ". . . .the least of our brethren. . . ." (Matt. 25:31-46), and if such work is not obvious to a visitor they might come to the conclusion that while we preach about love, we do not actually, on an "organizational" level, engage in charitable activity.

Offering food to the hungry, inviting people from the neighborhood in for coffee once a week, supporting or hosting a soup kitchen, visiting the sick or elderly and other charitable activities give an opportunity to those who might have a calling and desire to do such work to offer their time and energy to the parish, rather than some other religious or secular organization, as well as giving the poor, the marginalized, and the lonely contact with the Church.

The only thing necessary for parish renewal is true Christian love—unconditional, focused upon God and the neighbor, sacrificial and unselfish. A healthy parish serves the needs of the community—a dying parish expects the community to serve its needs. If we try to get new parishioners or keep our youth so that everything can remain the way we want it to be everything will inevitably fall apart. If, on the other hand, we concentrate on trying to fulfill God's commandments, trying to do His will, "parish renewal" will happen in and of itself.

Do we truly love and care for the people around us—the poor, those who live in the neighborhood of our church, and our non-religious friends and family members of whatever ethnic derivation—or are we concerned primarily with bricks and mortar, with "services," cultural events, and personal relationships? Is our love only *"in word or in tongue,"* or is it the real thing?■

Did You Hear?

". . . . the tongue is a fire, a world of iniquity . . . . no man can tame the tongue. It is an unruly evil, full of deadly poison. With it we bless our God and Father, and with it we curse men, who have been made in the similitude of God. Out of the same mouth proceed blessing and cursing. My brethren, these things ought not to be so" (James 3: 6, 8-10).

The phone rings:

"Hello?"

"Hello, Father. Did you hear?"

"Hear what?"

"Mrs. S___ had a stroke."

Mrs. S___ is a dedicated Church member whose whole family is involved in parish life. If something had happened to her I was sure someone would have called.

"Are you certain? Who told you this?"

"I don't want to say."

"I'll call you back in a minute," I said, and hung up. I immediately called Mrs. S___, who, miracle of miracles, answered the phone. We had a nice conversation, after which I called back the parishioner who had originally telephoned.

"I just spoke with Mrs. S___. I think you should call 'I don't want to say' and tell them to let Mrs. S___ know that she's had a stroke, because Mrs. S___ is under the impression that there is nothing wrong with her!"

This conversation (which really took place) is a relatively benign example of one of the greatest problems any Church, organization or community faces—rumor mongering.

The willful creation and spreading of rumors is destructive to the person who starts or spreads rumors, to those who are the object

15

of the rumor, and to the community. The person who starts or spreads rumors wastes time and creativity that could be put to constructive use; rumors are often derogatory or destructive to other people's reputations; and rumors always tear at the fabric of interpersonal relationships, for even when they are not aimed at destroying someone else's character they destroy the credibility of the person who spreads them.

Rumors are usually spread behind people's backs, which makes them doubly poisonous. Accusations are made with no chance for the accused to respond. Things which have no basis in reality—lies—become "facts" and take on a life of their own. There is a sociological principle which states that false beliefs become real in their consequences. Real people suffer, and often suffer greatly, because someone else has nothing better to do than sit on the phone or the Internet for hours every day exercising their imagination.

Why do people engage in such destructive activity? Usually in order to divert attention from themselves, or to avoid their personal feelings of inadequacy, sadness, or inferiority, or because they want to be "somebody" and find that this is more easily accomplished by tearing others down than by engaging in positive and constructive activities themselves.

How can we minimize this social and spiritual cancer?

The obvious first step is to never start rumors. Being involved in the central administration of the Church and present at all meetings of the Church leadership I am always amazed to hear stories from "out in the field" about what is allegedly happening on at the Metropolia, the priest transfers which are supposedly in the works, or the decisions which are purportedly being made which I have never heard discussed or proposed by anyone.

These stories start somewhere. The source is usually someone who instead could be praying, or reading the bible, or doing some other constructive spiritual work, but is captivated by the diabolical sensuality of being the first to say the words "Did you hear. . . ?"

If someone relates a rumor to me I should at least attempt to verify its accuracy, inquiring as to the source of the information. If the answer is "I do not want to say" it is probably wise to remember that what is good and true is not afraid of the light. Honest people are not secretive—thieves and murderers are. If I cannot trace a rumor back to the source there is probably a good reason.

I am sure many of us have suffered as a result of malicious gossip. How should we respond when false and malicious rumors are spread about us? When people maliciously gossip about us we are stuck between a rock and a hard place. Defending yourself against a rumor is often taken as proof of its truthfulness: "He would not react if it was not true, would he?" But not responding is usually interpreted as proof of its accuracy as well. When dealing with people who are not concerned about truth, who will not let facts get in the way, it is a no-win situation. So what do we do?

We follow the example of our Lord. He was slandered. He was called, among other things, a Samaritan, a drunkard, and Beelzebub! How did he respond? *"Like a lamb that is silent before its shearer he opened not His mouth"* (Isa.53:7-8). He not only refused to return evil for evil, He forgave, prayed and died for those who maligned Him. Though it is not an easy thing to do, it is the only thing that ultimately works.

The problem of rumor-mongering would be non-existent if we all just remembered a simple children's lesson. A well brought up child, before they say anything, is taught to ask themselves three simple questions: "Is it true? Is it kind? Is it necessary?" Before trying to be good Christians, perhaps we should just try to be good people. If something is not true why should I say it? If something is not kind do I have a good reason for repeating it? If something is not necessary why bother? We are taught as Christians that everything we do should be done in love. If non-Christians can regulate their conversation in accordance with these three small considerations, those purporting to be Christians should do at least as much.

"Is it true? Is it kind? Is it necessary?" We can follow this simple advice when choosing our words and avoid gossip, rumor-mongering, and the myriad of problems they cause. Or we can choose to ignore this simple advice and face the eternal consequences: *"For every idle word men may speak they will give account of it in the day of judgment. For by your words you will be justified, and by your words you will be condemned"* (Matt.12:36). ∎

That All Would Be One

Every normal human being knows that unity and oneness of mind is a blessing, something to be sought, treasured and cherished. One of the last things Christ begged of our Heavenly Father before His voluntary passion and death was unity for His disciples. We believe that it is Jesus' wish that His followers be one just as Jesus and the Father are one (cf. John.17:11).

We have all heard phrases such as "in unity there is strength." Before the anaphora of the Divine Liturgy the deacon intones *"Let us love one another so that with oneness of mind we may confess. . . ."* And yet how often it seems that in our governments, our societies, our communities, parishes, organizations and even our families the one thing that seems to be conspicuous by its absence is unity, concord, and harmony.

Is unity and oneness of mind even possible among human beings? If it is, how can it be achieved?

Jesus would not ask His Father for something which was impossible. But that which is possible is not necessarily easily achieved. We know that unity and oneness of mind is possible in the Church because it has been achieved. After Pentecost the apostles continued *". . . . daily with one accord. . . ."* (Acts 2:46). St. Paul tells the Galatians that they *". . . . are all one in Christ. . . ."* (Gal.3:28). Oneness and unity **are** possible—but only in Christ.

People attend Churches or are otherwise active in religious organizations for various reasons. Some attend simply to socialize. I remember a man telling me years ago, "Forgive me, Father, but the best part of the Church service is coffee hour afterwards!" He liked to socialize with his friends, and the fact that he had a hall full of potential clients for his business did not hurt either!

Other people belong to religious communities for cultural reasons. We live in a smorgasbord of religious culture where (at least in most big cities) people of various sexual orientations, ethnicities, socioeconomic classes, as well as devotees of fine (and sometimes not so fine) music, theater and literature can all "get validated" at the church, mosque, prayer hall or temple of their choice.

Language is a powerful unitive factor, especially among immigrant communities. People attend services in this or that congregation in order to worship God in a language they understand, or even in languages they do not understand but feel connected to for one reason or another. Certain congregations are about politics. It is the political orientation (whether the politics are of the "old country" or the "new country" variety) of the community that unites the congregants—except, of course, with those who hold different political views! Personal charisma can be another uniting factor. "I go to such and such Church because the priest is so dynamic!" The cult of personality is never good. Christianity is about Christ, not about who is in the pulpit.

There is nothing inherently wrong with socializing, culture, language, politics, or charisma. But none of these can hold a congregation together for long. Christian communities inevitably disintegrate unless their primary focus is on the person of Jesus Christ and the fulfilling of His Gospel teachings.

St. Paul teaches us that in the last days people will have a form of godliness, but will deny its power. (cf. 2 Tim. 3:5) Is this not what we have? We regard our Liturgies as nothing more than "ancient and colorful rituals." We make administrative decisions according to worldly logic, without prayer, fasting, or reference to Holy Scripture. We complain about factionalism in the congregation, but refuse to personally manifest Christ-like humility, forgiveness and repentance in trying to overcome destructive cliquishness. If we, who claim to be His disciples, actively sow discord or passively refuse to strive towards unity in the Church we oppose the will of God. And then, surprise of surprises, we experience conflict and divisiveness within the body of Christ.

It is axiomatic for Christians that God wants us to be united in love, peace, and harmony. Holy Scripture, the example of the saints, and the experience of the Church show us that this can only happen if we are united to, in and with Christ. There is no power or person other than Jesus Christ who can unite the native Ukrainian or English or French or Russian or Hungarian speakers; the German or Russian or Canadian or Ukrainian or Irish or American or Polish born; the farmers, the professors, the teachers, the nurses, the doctors, the lawyers, the accountants, the scientists, the retirees; the teenagers, the children, the parents, the grandparents; the converts, the mixed-marriage couples, the blacks, the whites, the Asians and the aboriginals of the Church. None. Not culture, not language, not social interaction, not "super priest," nothing and no one except Jesus Christ. So we have to ask ourselves, both personally and collectively, one simple question: "What do we want?" Do we want unity for our families, our parishes, and our Church? If so then we have to seek it in Christ, no matter what our background is, what melodies we sing in Church or what language we speak. We must offer ourselves, our families and our congregations to Christ totally and exclusively, in every possible way.

One question remains, however. If we do not in our heart of hearts want the unity that God desires for us and for His Church, then what are we doing here? ■

Nasty People

You know who I am talking about. Most parishes have one. The woman who is very pleasant, even complimentary, to your face, but when your back is turned sticks the dagger in. And turns it. Or the man whose avowed purpose in life (it seems) is to make sure that everyone entering the Church hears about how bad the priest is, how dishonest the parish council is, and how impious the parishioners are. Who has not been affected by the pathological gossip, whose self-esteem seems to grow in direct proportion to the amount of pain and discomfort they can cause others by spreading malicious and destructive rumors? And we cannot forget the clergyman who uses his position to lord it over others, manipulate his parishioners for personal benefit, or malign his brother priests behind their backs in order to deflect attention from his own failings and inadequacies.

Whether we want to admit it or not, these and other types of nasty people are the neighbor Jesus tells us we must love. (cf. Matt. 5:43-48). And our Lord, wanting to give us the best possible opportunity to prove our faith by our deeds, often puts these people where we cannot overlook them—sometimes in the pew right next to us.

It is no secret that one of the biggest turn-offs to those seeking a parish community as well as the children of devout parishioners is the hypocritical, antagonistic and downright unpleasant attitude of certain "Christians." Visitors enter a Church, encounter one of these nasty people, and come out after Liturgy or coffee hour thinking "If this is what attending this Church does to a person then I don't want any part of it!" Though this response is logical, it is based on a couple of misconceptions. First of all, maybe the nasty person they met is of such a lineage of hate and dysfunction that just getting to the point of being ornery, difficult and unpleasant was a major accomplishment. Such a "difficult" person may actually be much more praiseworthy in the sight of God than someone who was born with a pleasant personality yet cares neither for God or neighbor. Secondly, we have to determine whether such a nasty person was actually "walking the walk" as Christians at all. Many people who are active in their parishes and consider themselves good Christians in reality have absolutely no relationship with Jesus Christ. It is usually easy to spot them—they do not seem to be terribly interested in spending time with God, for one. I am not talking about being present for Liturgy, as the Liturgy is a good place for a person who does not really care about God to "hide." I'm talking about prayer. Private, contemplative, faithful daily prayer, as well as the frequent and regular reading of scripture is usually absent from the lives of such people. They usually do not fast, either. They will often say things like: "Father, since when are we forbidden to eat meat on Friday? Is that not a stupid rule? I do not need to follow stupid rules!"

What right does a person who does not pray, fast, help the poor, read the bible, donate generously to their parish and regularly receive the holy mysteries of confession and communion have to call themselves a Christian at all? While the long-time parishioner might know that Mr. K. or Mrs. N. do not actually live Christian lives the infrequent guest or parish visitor does not have the benefit of this knowledge, and so comes to the incorrect but valid conclusion that all the people in the parish are, well, nasty hypocrites.

Yes, there are nasty people in this world. We see them in our schools, our workplaces, and our Churches. When dealing with such people there are two fundamental things which we as Christians must never forget. First of all, we should always be searching our own hearts, analyzing our own actions, and trying to discern whether we are not being nasty or mean-spirited to others. It is a psychological truth that the very behaviors we condemn in others are often the same behaviors we ourselves engage in. In the words of St. Isaac of Syria, *". . . . help me to see my own sins, and not to judge my brother. . . ."* Secondly, we must remember that our faith is authentic only insofar as it is manifested in our actions. As St. Ignatius Brianchianinov writes in <u>The Arena</u>: *"All the sorrows and sufferings caused us by people never come to us except with God's permission for our essential good. . . . They are indispensable, in order that we may have occasion to forgive our neighbors and so receive forgiveness of our own sins. They are indispensable, in order that we may discern the Providence of God watching over us and acquire a living faith in God. . . . They are indispensable, in order that we may acquire love for our enemies, for it is love that finally purifies the heart of the poison of malice and makes it capable of loving God and of receiving that special, abundant grace from God. . . . love for our enemies is the highest rung on the ladder of love for our neighbors, through which we enter the vast palace of love for God."* ■

My Life for Thine

All life is based on the principle: "my life for thine."

The natural world shows us that plants give up their lives so animals might live, insects give up their lives to feed birds or bats, domestic animals give their lives that humans might be nourished.

Human society is no different. Parents sacrifice their lives, figuratively and sometimes even literally, for their children. Children give their lives for their parents. Soldiers offer their lives for their country. Indeed, without sacrificing our lives for each other in the opportunities, both great and small, which are presented to us daily, there simply would be no human society, no family, no life.

"My life for thine"—this is, as well, the principle of all spiritual life. Our Lord teaches us that ". . . .*unless a grain of wheat dies and is buried in the ground it does not bring forth fruit*" (John 12:24).

A physical manifestation of this truth is the literal grain of wheat that must die so that I might have my toast or cereal in the morning. A spiritual manifestation would be the crowns bestowed upon a couple at their wedding. These crowns symbolize the crowns of the martyrs, who are the paradigmatic Christians— those who give their life for Christ. The husband and wife are symbolically shown that the married state involves nothing less than sacrificing one's life for one's spouse. Unless selfishness and egoism die Christian marriage cannot grow and blossom.

Priests are called to give their lives for the faithful. As our Lord says, *"The good shepherd gives his life for the sheep"* (John 10:11). Before ordination bishops and priests agree to serve wherever they are assigned, which often means leaving family, friends, and familiar surroundings. They understand that their job is a "24/7" proposition, that they are always on call, and that as fathers they are obliged to take responsibility for their flock before God, living the same sacrificial life a good "biological" father would live for his children.

Lay ministers and Church leaders are no different. Holding a position of responsibility in the Church—whether pastoral or administrative—means giving of our time, our energy, our loving care, our patience, longsuffering, talents. The parish council member, the lay minister visiting the sick and shut-in, the Sunday school teacher, the person working in a mission serving the poor and homeless are all living examples of "my life for thine."

All our self-made problems, whether social, financial, ecclesial or spiritual, can be traced back to someone, somewhere, who refuses to take responsibility for others, to actually put the words "my life for thine" into practice. Pastors who desire the privileges and honor of their priestly office while shunning their God-given responsibilities is a good example. Parish council members or leaders of lay organizations who wish to dictate without actually doing is another. Parishioners who want access to a beautiful temple with beautiful services and the comfort of good pastoral care but are unwilling to sacrifice their fair share of time, work, or money are guilty as well.

Christ's great law of love tells us that we must love God with our whole heart, our whole soul, our whole mind, and all our strength (i.e., with our material possessions), and love our neighbor as ourselves. (cf. Mark 12:30-31) We are immediately struck by the fact that our concentration, our "preoccupation," is to be directed outward, toward God and neighbor, not inward, to the self. In other words, "my life for thine."

This is the teaching of Christ. This is the example of our Lord. This is the message of the Cross. If we call ourselves Christians this must be our own personal example. Every time we make the sign of the Cross we must remember this teaching. "My life for thine." We are reading these words because our forebears—both spiritual and biological—lived these words. If we truly wish to pass our faith to our descendants and to the world we have no choice but to do the same. ∎

What a bad priest!

I know a young priest. He is dedicated, hard working, God-loving, and cares deeply for his flock. He discovered one day that an elderly parishioner had died, and was being buried by a neighboring priest. When he called the priest to confirm this, he was told that it was true, and that the family had asked him to do so. Father then called the family and asked them why they had asked the priest of another parish to bury their mother, and was told: "while she was in the nursing home you never visited her."

Here we have two problems. The first problem regards the priest who agreed to perform a funeral for the parishioner of another parish. This is forbidden. Priests are only permitted to minister to the members of a different parish with the express agreement and foreknowledge of the pastor of the parish, and/or the permission of the eparchial Bishop. So the priest who agreed to perform the funeral without the knowledge or consent of the pastor of the deceased was blatantly flouting Church order and discipline.

The second problem is more complex. Our young, dedicated pastor had tried on many occasions to visit the deceased, when she was still at home as well as when she was taken to the nursing home. He had tried to call the deceased, and left phone messages with the children asking if a visit was desired, messages which received no response whatever. Never having received a request for a visit, not having had his calls even acknowledged, not knowing which nursing home she was in (and he only knew about her being in a nursing home from third-hand sources), he found it somewhat unfair to be treated the way he was.

I have had similar experiences. And I think I had situations where I may have unintentionally offended someone in some way: speaking Ukrainian when they wanted to speak English, or vice versa; not visiting them in the hospital when I had not received a call and their name did not appear on the "religion list" in the lobby; not noticing or greeting someone at a Church or community function; having a beard which is too long/too short, or simply just having a beard. The problem is that people often do not say "father, such-and-such happened, and I got upset. What happened? Were you ignoring me?" They just bear a grudge, and call another priest to bury them!

This is not right. It is unfair, and it is unchristian. Conflicts, mistakes, oversights, and missed opportunities are a regular part of our life, but we must resolve them. In the Gospel of St. Matthew Jesus says: *"Agree with your adversary quickly, while you are on the way with him, lest your adversary deliver you to the judge, the judge hand you over to the officer, and you be thrown into prison"* (5:25). "The way" is this life, the judge is God, and the officer is the devil who wishes to bind us forever in hell. The only condition upon which our own forgiveness from God is based is found in the very next chapter: *". . . forgive us our trespasses as we forgive those who trespass against us. . . ."* (Matt. 6:12).

The Church, understanding both the teaching of Our Lord as well as sinful human nature, has given us a particular means to help us resolve these and other similar conflicts. It is a concrete manifestation of forgiveness, related to but different from confession. It is the first service of Lent, served usually on the evening of Cheese-fare Sunday. It is called Forgiveness Vespers.

The service is very beautiful and moving. Before the service starts the black or purple lenten coverings are placed on the altar and throughout the Church, with the bright Sunday coverings being lightly placed overtop so that they can be removed easily during the service. Vespers begins like a normal Sunday evening service, but when it comes time for the Prokimen the priest or deacon intones the lenten Sunday Prokimen: *"Turn not away Thy face from Thy child for I am afflicted. Hear me speedily. Draw near unto my soul and deliver it!"*

During the mournful singing of the Prokimen and verses the royal doors and curtain are closed, the bright altar and table coverings are removed, the priest takes off his bright vestments and puts on a dark epitrachil and we move into lent. The service continues as lenten vespers, concluding with the lenten troparia and prostrations, the prayer of St. Ephraim the Syrian, and lenten dismissal. Following the dismissal, the liturgical books state that the priest is to preach a sermon about forgiveness and the need for mutual forgiveness, and then all present perform the rite of mutual forgiveness.

This rite of mutual forgiveness is performed daily in monasteries, after Compline. It consists of the priest or main celebrant kneeling before the assembled congregation and asking forgiveness for the sins he may have committed, those of knowledge, of ignorance, everything. The assembled faithful reply: "God forgives. Forgive us father, and pray for us." The faithful then kneel and ask forgiveness, saying "Forgive us, father, all our sins, whether in thought, in word, in deed, in knowledge, or in ignorance." or some similar words. After the priest's expression of forgiveness the faithful approach one by one to the main celebrant—first clergy, then servers, singers, and faithful. They perform a prostration in front of each other, the priest or person greeting saying: "Forgive me (*name*, or *brother*, or *sister*) and pray for me, a sinner." The person approaching replies: "God forgives. Forgive me, and pray for me." They then stand and exchange the kiss of peace, three times on the cheeks. The first person in line then stands to the priest's right, the next to their right, and in this way everyone present exchanges forgiveness with everyone else.

While this is going on one or several of the singers will quietly be singing the Paschal Stychyry "Let God arise. . . ." These remind us of what we are preparing for—God's Resurrection, our Resurrection, Pascha. It is during these same verses that we exchange the Paschal kiss on Easter Sunday morning. Lent is a long, 50 day journey, filled with hardships, requiring the help and support of those who love us. We begin this journey with a kiss, and end it with a kiss.

I am sure that at this point many of you are saying to yourselves: "What in the world is he talking about? I have never heard of this! He must be making this up!" I assure you I am not. Just because you have never heard of something does not mean it is not true, neither does it mean that it is not necessary, or desirable, or beneficial.

Others may be asking themselves: "Why do I need to ask forgiveness of people I have not offended, even from total strangers?" Every one of us is a sinner. If we think we are not sinners the Scriptures say we delude ourselves. Sin is always destructive. Sin is not only hurtful to God, it is always hurtful to us, and to others. So no matter how we have sinned we have hurt others, both those we know and those we do not know.

It is likewise important to remember that Christians do not believe only in sin, but also in forgiveness. We not only ask forgiveness, we extend forgiveness. That person you are bowing in front of might need your forgiveness for something you do not even know about. Extending forgiveness is a God-like act. Being present for the Forgiveness Vespers and taking part in the rite of mutual forgiveness permits us to concretely manifest our two natures, confessing our sinful humanity, and showing our divine calling.

Parish communities, like families, often experience conflict, misunderstanding, and friction. Every community does. When this social and human disintegration continues unchecked it often leads to major problems. I am sure all of us know of parishes where, due to the sinful self-righteousness and pride of individual faithful or clergy, "parties" are formed, battle lines are drawn, and people who consider themselves "good Christians" not only do not talk to one another, but actively "eat and devour" each other for real or perceived slights.

Such a parish is doomed to failure. The hypocrisy of such action is obvious even to non-Christians. Forgiveness vespers is a control mechanism which reminds us, if only once a year, that every other member of my community is my brother or sister, that I am just a sinner like everyone else, that the real test of our faith is how we treat our worst enemies. Christians love even their enemies. If there is anyone at all on the face of this earth whom I cannot forgive, I have no business approaching for confession or communion. I have no business hoping that God will forgive me. I might even ask myself "what am I doing in Church in the first place?

If your parish serves Forgiveness Vespers go. Take your family. Do not be shy. If it does not ask the priest to do so. Even if it is only you and him present for the service you will have done something very important and good. If he refuses find the nearest parish that does and attend there. It will be the beginning of a great lent, and an even better eternity. ∎

PERSONAL SPIRITUALITY

Prayer Rules!

The chain, as the saying goes, is only as strong as its weakest link. If we wish to have a strong Church, we must have strong parishes. If we wish to have strong parishes, we must have strong families. If we wish to have strong families, we must individually have strong faith, and in order to have strong faith we must pray.

With the exception of regular and frequent attendance at Divine Services—Sunday and Holy day Liturgies, Vespers, Orthros, akathists and other services—there is no more important factor in our development as Christians than our personal life of prayer. It is not an exaggeration to say that no one can claim to be a Christian if they do not engage in regular, personal prayer. Prayer is something that no one can do in our place, anymore than it is possible for someone to repent in our place. People can pray for us, but no one can pray instead of us. God has children, but no grandchildren.

In our hectic, busy and complicated world, where it seems that we do not have time for much of anything, how should we approach this most important of Christian deeds? What principles are necessary to observe, what compromises are permitted or not permitted in arranging our prayer-life properly?

The Rule of Prayer. The particular ordering of our personal, daily prayers is referred to as our "rule of prayer." Interestingly, the word "rule" can have several different meanings. It can, for instance, refer to an ordinance or directive, to a measurement (as in "ruler" or "slide-rule"), or it can refer to governance, as in a King ruling over a country. It is worthy of note that all these definitions have an important place in our understanding of the rule of prayer—it is the sign if my allegiance to the King; it refers to measurement in regards to the length of my daily prayers; and refers to governance insofar as prayer is a rule I must follow if I wish to be a Christian.

Simply put, the rule of prayer is the specific order of prayers prayed by a Christian during the course of a day. It will normally include prayers upon rising or morning prayers; prayers before sleep or evening prayers; prayers before meals; and may include other prayers during the day and/or prayers on the prayer-rope (chotki or prayer rope).

It is commonly accepted that every Orthodox Christian should have a particular rule of prayer which they follow religiously (pun intended). The rule of prayer is different for clergy, monastics, mothers, fathers, children, etc. The particular rule of prayer which we follow should ideally reflect our spiritual maturity, our state in life, and take into account our lifestyle and family situation.

The golden rule regarding our prayer life is the law of consistency. It is more important to be able to set aside 5 minutes every morning and every evening for simple, heartfelt, unrushed prayer than to take on a rule of prayer which will take an hour to complete, and which I might only fulfill once or twice a week. In our prayer life, as in most everything, it is quality and not quantity that counts.

Where should I pray? Many people have the mistaken ideas that we only go to Church to pray, or that we go to Church only to pray. While prayer is an important part of what we do in Church, we actually attend services in Church for the purpose of worshiping God. Jesus states in the Gospel: ". . . . *when you pray, go into your room, and when you have shut your door, pray to your Father who is in the secret place; and your Father who sees in secret will reward you openly"* (Matt. 6:6). This teaching is maintained in the Orthodox Church. An Orthodox home will have a particular corner or wall, normally the eastern corner or wall, where the icons will be displayed. This would be the normal place for familial prayer. Other personal prayers might be said in a quiet place, perhaps in our own rooms, standing or sitting in front of the icons with the door closed. Whether we are at home, at work or traveling, the main criterion regarding where we pray is that it be quiet and reasonably private.

Morning prayer. Any good prayer book will have a section entitled "morning prayers" or "prayers upon arising." These are not hard to find. The most important and difficult aspect of morning prayers is usually not which prayers are said, but waking up on time! Having good intentions to pray for five minutes every morning will bear no fruit if I do not wake up at least five minutes earlier every morning, and in fact might cause both me and my family grief. Prayer upon arising—giving the first minutes of the day to God—is an ancient and beneficial Christian exercise, a discipline that each and every one of us should personally practice.

Regarding which prayers might be said, the general outline in any good Orthodox prayer book is relatively similar. We begin with the usual beginning (opening blessing, prayer to the Holy Spirit, Trisagion, prayer to the Holy Trinity, and the Lord's prayer), followed by the troparia upon arising, the prayer of St. Basil the Great, Psalm 50, the Nicene Creed, and then a greater or lesser number of other prayers. Just this basic beginning, from the opening blessing till the Creed, can easily be recited prayerfully in five minutes, and is a good beginning for those who do not currently practice any morning prayers. If done devoutly, consistently, and with attention it will bring great benefit to the life of the one praying. The simple psychological benefit of beginning the day in peace (and no one can truly pray if they are not first at peace) will bring its own benefits to our own life and the lives of those around us.

Evening prayers. A Slavic prayer book (whether Ukrainian, Russian, or Serbian) will tend to follow a format for evening prayers which is similar to the format for the morning prayers, the difference occurring in the text of the prayers themselves. Byzantine (Greek, Syrian, Antiochian, or Romanian) prayer books will often give the text of Small Compline where we would expect to see evening prayers. Compline is the service which is chanted after the evening meal in monasteries, and contains psalms, hymns and prayers before sleep. Either of these practices is beneficial, it is simply up to the individual, under the direction of their spiritual father, to decide which of these approaches is best for them and to follow it consistently.

Prayers during the day. Generally the prayers said during the day are short and informal. Most prayer books contain specific prayers for specific daily needs—whether it be a simple "God, help me" or Lord, bless!" before we begin a task, whether it be the prayers designated for students before or after lessons, or any other prayers applicable to my station in life, we can write these prayers on separate pieces of paper or memorize them and utilize them in the course of the day to ask God's help and blessing in all we do.

All of us, no matter where we are, should ask God's blessing before we eat (the prayers for the blessing of food can be found in any prayer book) and cross ourselves. Whether we are in a restaurant, at work, in the school cafeteria, at the food court in the mall, or anywhere else we should remember Christ's words *"But whoever denies Me before men, him I will also deny before My Father who is in heaven"* (Matt.10:33), and not be ashamed to pray and cross ourselves before we eat.

The Jesus Prayer. Many Orthodox Christians follow, as part of their rule of prayer, a particular and very beneficial way of praying known as the "Jesus prayer." This is a short prayer, consisting of the words *"Lord, Jesus Christ, Son of God, have mercy upon me the sinner."* This is an ancient prayer, composed of two parts—the glorification of Jesus as the Christ, Lord, and Son of God, combined with our basic human prayer and need that God have mercy upon us. This prayer can be recited using a prayer rope to count the number of repetitions. A member of the faithful, for example, might have a rule of prayer which encompasses a particular selection of morning and evening prayers, and 50 repetitions of the Jesus Prayer on the prayer rope. This prayer on the prayer rope might be done in conjunction with, or apart from the morning or evening prayers, but it is especially important that it be done in a quiet, unhurried manner, preferably in a quiet place.

The Jesus Prayer is a very beneficial method of prayer, but one which should be done under the direction of someone who is experienced in this method of prayer. There are many good books available on the Jesus prayer, but books cannot look us in the eye and relate their contents to our individual circumstances. As we all know, others often have a clearer picture of our personal strengths and weaknesses than we do ourselves. We must be especially wary of pride as a motivation for prayer (or for anything else), and so while the advice and direction of a holy, prayerful spiritual father or experienced monk or nun is important regarding our prayer life in general, it is especially important regarding our practice of the Jesus Prayer.

Other methods of prayer. Two other types of prayer which are commonly practiced are intercessory prayer and "improvisational" or "free" prayer. Intercessory prayer is simply prayer for a specific person or intention. We might pray for someone's health, for the repose of their soul, for their quick recovery, for success in school or at work, etc. The common way of doing this is by mentioning the name of a specific person or persons in a short petition, for example, *"Lord Jesus Christ, give health to your servant(s). . . ,"* or *"Grant rest, O Lord, to the soul of your servant(s). . . ."* In praying for ourselves we can simply adjust the words of the Jesus Prayer to reflect our intention, for example "Lord Jesus Christ, help me complete my work successfully." Such intercessory or supplicatory prayer is good and necessary. These types of petitions for our family, friends and other intentions fit well at the end of our formal morning and evening prayers, as well as during the day as the need arises.

Being surrounded by various protestant sects, we no doubt have come across people who do not believe in structured prayer. They "pray as the spirit moves them." This type of free or improvisational prayer is not bad or evil in and of itself, but it is not generally recommended for just anyone. Why? Imagine an 8 year old who wants to be a jazz saxophonist, and has been given a saxophone and taught to play notes on it. In order for this young person to learn to improvise they do not begin by playing whatever notes they wish in whatever order they wish, for they would only make noise and become discouraged. First they must learn scales, music theory, how different musical keys relate to one another, standard musical phrases, etc. This takes years. Only at the end of this structured education do they begin to be able to successfully improvise.

The Church has always followed the same logical and beneficial approach. We begin to pray not by using our own words, but God's words. We do not "grandstand." We say the Our Father. We recite the angelic salutation to Mary. We read the psalms. We pray the prayers of the saints. Only after years of repeating God's prayers will we begin to understand the true depth and meaning of prayer, or to see that prayer is not something which we do to make ourselves feel good. Prayer which is centered on us is not prayer at all, but simply diabolical delusion, and so rather than beating my own path through the bush I follow the (prayer) path trodden by Our Lord and the saints.

Families with children. Parents have a special responsibility as far as the prayer life of their children is concerned. In addition to their own rule of prayer, parents should pray with their children both morning and evening. While the personal and familial prayer of a parent might be combined to a greater or lesser degree, it is especially important that children learn to pray every day, morning and evening, from their youngest years. The prayers themselves should obviously be short and easily understood, and expanded as the child grows. The example of a parent or parents praying both with their children and also alone is a lesson which children will never forget.

Why is prayer important? There are many who might say that our personal prayer is at best a crutch and at worst a waste of time. There are those who would say that rather than sitting home praying we should be doing something "useful." Did not Jesus say, after all, that we would be judged on whether or not we fed the hungry, clothed the naked, visited the sick and those in prison?

Yes, He did, but He also went out into the desert to pray alone. He left crowds of people who had come to be healed and taught in order that He might have time to commune with His Father in prayer. He did not say "I am above the need for prayer and worship." but He attended and took active part in Divine Services and spent time (probably much more than any of us ever will) in prayer and fasting.

If Our Lord gives us this example, we who bear His name must follow it. Those who follow a regular rule of prayer do not need to be convinced of its value, and so the only answer we can give to the question: "do I really need to do this?" is: "try it." Anyone, following a reasonable rule of prayer for 6 months, will see the value, benefits and blessings it brings. They will find that rather than taking time away from "useful" deeds like helping the poor, elderly or infirm they will (almost magically) find more time for this important work. Indeed, the argument can be made that Jesus was able to teach, preach and heal as much as He did not in spite of the amount of time He spent in prayer, but precisely because of the time He spent in prayer.

We all face challenges, difficulties and even conflict in our Churches, families, and communities. There is ultimately only one person who can address these problems—me. Following a rule of prayer consistently and humbly will bring a degree of peace, stress relief, and simplicity—not to mention God's blessing and wisdom—to our personal lives. There is no surer way to draw closer to God and strengthen our parishes, families and communities as well. ∎

A Christian Ending to Our Life

At every service we pray for "a Christian ending to our life". Priests often get called to hospitals to serve the "last rites" over dying people, some of whom are very devout members of the Church, others whom they have never met nor even heard of before. Everyone seems to understand that the time of death is a time when God's presence is especially necessary and desirable. What do we really ask for when we pray for "a Christian ending to our life?"

We are taught that the human person is composed of body and soul. Death is the temporary separation of the body and soul. Even as the body is buried in the earth, the soul continues its existence and stands before God for judgement. Between the time of the death of the individual and the general resurrection—the "end of the world," when everyone's souls will be reunited to a new, resurrected body and we will stand before Christ to be judged—we are taught that the soul feels, to some incomplete degree, either the joy of the saints or the pain of hell, and that after the general resurrection, when body and soul will again be united, we will feel either the full pain of hell or the total joy of the saints.

We are taught that in order to experience the joy of the saints we must use our time here on earth to follow the path of salvation which has been shown to us by God, much like a young dancer, ice-skater or athlete, if they wish to achieve success in their chosen field, must follow the direction and teaching of their teacher or coach and not just make it up as they go along or "express their own unique creativity." As the athlete experiences her examination when she takes the playing field and the dancer when he takes the stage, every Christian will experience their most important examination when they stand before Christ at their death. Consequently, as the athlete or artist must take great care to prepare themselves properly immediately before they are to perform, so the time immediately before our death is perhaps the most important time in our life.

We often hear of the "last rites." From the standpoint of Orthodox Christianity this is at best a misguided or imprecise idea. As we prepare for death God has given us three main sacramental acts which are to ease our transition into the heavenly kingdom: the holy mysteries of Confession and Communion; the holy mystery of anointing or the "Oil of Prayer;" and the prayers at the separation of the soul and the body.

Confession and Communion. A person who is about to die, if they do nothing else, should receive the mysteries of Confession and the Eucharist. This is one reason why it is important not to wait till the last minute, when a person is on a respirator and cannot talk or is already unconscious. No one can be confessed or communed unless they are conscious and relatively coherent. The forgiveness of sins we receive through a good, honest and open confession is much more important than all the pain-killers in the world, for it is one of the only things which can keep us from the eternal pain of hell. The union with Christ which we achieve through partaking of the Body and Blood of Our Lord in the Eucharist is that which gives us peace of mind and comfort in the difficult task of making our final farewells to our loved ones and in the terrible moment of death. We pray at every Liturgy for ". . . *a Christian ending to our life, painless, blameless and peaceful."* Holy Confession and Holy Communion make this possible. We are taught that Holy Communion is "the medicine of immortality." Anyone who is gravely sick or in danger of death should receive Confession and Communion as soon as possible. These Holy Mysteries are the sign of a Christian life (which is why we always approach at least once a year), and they are likewise the mark of a Christian death.

Holy Unction. As we read through the beautiful prayers of the anointing service we see that the prayers offered are not for a Christian death, but for the forgiveness of sins and the healing of the body and soul of the person being anointed. It is a service for those who wish to get well, not those about to die. Consequently, waiting till someone is dying before calling a priest so that he might serve this mystery is perhaps not the best thing to do. It would be much better if all of us, upon being informed that we have a serious illness, asked the priest to serve this mystery as soon as possible, while we are still strong enough to join our prayers to the prayers of the Church.

Likewise, we see that Holy Unction should be served if at all possible in Church, preferably with several priests concelebrating. The reason is found in the first epistle reading of the service. *"Is anyone among you suffering? Let him pray. . . . Is anyone among you sick? Let him call for the elders of the Church, and let them pray over him, anointing him with oil in the name of the Lord. And the prayer of faith will save the sick, and the Lord will raise him up. And if he has committed sins, he will be forgiven. Confess your trespasses to one another, and pray for one another, that you may be healed"* (1 James, 5:13-16). The word "elders" in Greek is *presbyteroi*—the word from which we get the term *presbyter* or priest. Ideally 7 priests should concelebrate this mystery together.

It is unfortunate that Holy Unction is rarely served in its full form—most often it is simply the blessing of the oil and the anointing itself, what in the book of needs is referred to as the order "to be used when in danger of death." This is a beautiful service which, when approached with faith on the part of both the sick person and those present, is very powerful. It consists of the opening prayers, the blessing of the oil itself, 7 epistle and gospel readings followed immediately by 7 anointings (done by 7 different priests if present), and then, before the dismissal, the gospel book is opened and placed, text facing down, over the head of the ill person and the main celebrant reads a beautiful prayer asking God Himself to heal the sick person, saying *"I lay not my sinful hand on the head of (him or her) who has come to You in iniquities and asks of You, through me, remission of sins, but through Your strong and mighty hand which is in this Holy Gospel held over the head of Thy servant. . . ."* Even in an abbreviated form, with only one priest serving (and this is usually the case due to time and distance constraints) the service can be very beautiful—especially if the family of the sick person are believers and join their prayers to the prayers of the priest.

Prayers at the parting of the soul from the body. When a person is on the verge of death we have a beautiful set of prayers in the book of needs which are to be read. It is in the form of a canon and basically is a petition to God to forgive the sins and grant a peaceful death to the one who is dying, and permit their soul to separate from their body peacefully. These prayers are rarely read for several reasons. Certain people hold a secularized outlook and do not see prayer as beneficial. In addition to this we are surrounded by non-Orthodox who have different practices, and the force of assimilation causes us to see our Faith in the light of these non-Orthodox teachings and practices. Since the Catholics or Protestants do not have these prayers at the parting of the body and soul we tend to forget that they exist. Lastly, it is often the case that family members do not want to admit that someone they love is dying, and so to pray the prayers at death would be too difficult. This is unfortunate, because for to those who understand what our mortal life is about and have walked with God here below these prayers can be a great comfort.

It occasionally happens that a priest is called to the deathbed of someone he does not know, someone who might not be Orthodox, or someone who has left the Church. We understand that Confession, Communion, and Unction are Holy Mysteries of the Church, and as such are not to be performed for the non-Orthodox, nor for those who have consciously denied the Faith. The family wishes the priest to do something, but what can he do? It must be emphasized over and over again that the holy mysteries are not to be looked upon with desperation as a miracle cure to be requested when the doctors have done all that they can do. Nor are they to be looked upon as magic, as if the priest could show up, say some special words, sprinkle some water or wipe some oil on the dying person, magically transforming them from a sinner into a saint so that they will go straight to heaven. God will do his part—but we have to do ours as well.

John the Baptist preached confession and repentance of sins. Jesus began His ministry with the preaching of repentance. The Church exists to help us repent. As we approach death this is of extreme importance. Repentance is a conscious renunciation of the devil and all service to him, a renunciation of all our sinful acts, and a heartfelt promise to God to change our sinful way of life. This is why it is extremely important that the priest be called when the sick person is still conscious, coherent, and able to make a good confession, able to receive the mysteries with faith. The priest cannot repent for anyone else except himself, and to expect the priest to "do something" for a person who is unconscious or under the effects of painkillers is unreasonable. The only thing he might do in this circumstance is to pray, and to try to comfort the family. We must remember that it is never too late to repent—and God wishes that everyone be saved. No matter who is dying, no matter what their sins are, whether public or private, we are taught that true repentance and reconciliation to the Church through the Holy Mysteries will bring salvation. This is the reason that we should never wait till the last minute to call the priest, and why we especially should not be afraid to call the priest to the bedside of anyone who is gravely ill for fear of "traumatizing" the patient.

One final point remains to be made. Every one of us is dying. We are closer to death now than we were when we began reading this book. Life, as we know, is a terminal illness. It is no surprise that the most important of our acts in preparing for death is approaching for Confession and Communion, for these are the central mysteries of our faith during our earthly life, the most concrete signs of our belonging to God and His Church. While it is good for someone to repent on their deathbed, it is even better to repent throughout one's entire life. None of us knows when we will die—today, tomorrow, or years from now. But we do know that those who are always prepared stand a better chance of success than those who constantly postpone their preparation, whether for school, for work, or for death.

Saint Nikolai Velmirovic, in a homily about the Holy Mystery of Unction, states: *"Oh, my brethren, how ineffable is God's goodness! What has the Lord not done for us? What more could we desire? He has foreseen all our needs and provided medicine for them in advance. He only seeks from us that we believe in Him and fulfill His commandments. Is it not blind of us, and shameful, that we often carry out the directions of doctors, mortal men like ourselves, more carefully and conscientiously than we do those of God immortal? O all-gracious Lord, shatter the stone of our hearts with the power of Thy grace; that we may, before our last hour, show Thee the gratitude we owe Thee, O our gracious and most wise God."* ■

On Fasting

The Orthodox Church has rules. Rules about how we dress, about how we cross ourselves, about when we can and cannot be married, about how to bow, how to stand, about our moral life and about our human interactions. It is not surprising, since we follow an unbroken 2,000 year tradition.

All of these little things that we do are good and valuable, but simply because there are so many of them we often have a tendency to ignore many of them. "I'll just do the main things," many people say. The problem is that when it comes to a discussion of what the "main things" are, it usually ends up being the personal opinion of the person involved which is the deciding factor. We have many people in the Orthodox Church who honestly and guilelessly believe that the "main thing" is to attend services a few times a year, not kill anyone (except perhaps through abortion), and be a "nice guy." The only problem is that this is not Christianity.

Fasting is one of the things which has generally fallen by the wayside in our North American Orthodox life. Although fasting is a serious matter for both Christ (read the 6th chapter of St. Matthew's Gospel, for example) and the Church (one of the earliest Christian documents, the <u>Didache</u>, or Teaching of the Twelve Apostles, gives specific instructions regarding fasting on Wednesdays and Fridays) we, in our twenty-first century wisdom, often feel free to abandon this practice.

According to the practice of the Orthodox Church, which has been fine tuned under the guidance of the Holy Spirit by 2,000 years of trial and error, Orthodox Christians should refrain from eating meat and dairy products as follows: a) on all Wednesdays and Fridays during the year (with the exception of the four fast free weeks); b) during the entire duration of the Great Fast, the Nativity Fast, the Apostles' Fast and the Dormition Fast, and c) on the feasts of the

Beheading of St. John the Baptist and the Exaltation of the Holy Cross. Fasting consists not only of refraining from meat and dairy products, but in limiting the amount of food consumed, refraining from excessive talking, gossip, loud music and dancing.

One of the excuses given for ignoring the rule of fasting is that "we are not legalistic about our fasting." Being legalistic is a very specific attitude. It means that we think that if we fulfill this or that rule we will be saved. This is obviously false. We do not fast, or pray, or help the poor, or attend services because if we do so we will automatically go to heaven. Although we have many rules, we should never do anything which is "legalistic." The Old Testament Law was replaced with the Grace of Christ. In practice, however, when people say they are not being legalistic about fasting it often means "I know we have rules about fasting, but I do not think there is anything wrong with ignoring them."

To see the absurdity of this attitude let us look at other spheres of our life. Let us not be "legalistic" about our marriages. "Sure, I made a vow never to commit adultery, but I am not going to be legalistic about it!" and the marriage is destroyed. Let us not be legalistic about prayer or the sacramental life. "I am not concerned about praying morning and evening, and all these rules about receiving Holy Communion are stupid!" and my relationship with God is destroyed. "I am not going to interpret the red light at the corner legalistically, it is just there as a guide for those who need it" and my car, and perhaps my life, are "negatively impacted."

Rules exist for a reason, and if I do not understand why a particular rule exists, I should try to find out. Fasting is central to our spiritual discipline. Every religion practices some type of fasting. There is no more fundamental act than putting food in our mouths. If we can control what and how much we put into our mouth chances are we have the discipline to be disciples. How could I stand up to those who would persecute, torture or kill me for my faith if I am not able to do something as simple as keep the fast? How can I expect my son or daughter to say no to sex in the back seat of a car on Saturday night if they cannot say no to a hamburger on Friday? Fasting does not save us, but it does help develop the discipline necessary to make those important decisions which do.

Fasting gives us spiritual strength. This is reiterated again and again in the Holy Scriptures. Jesus fasts and prays before beginning His ministry. He tells the apostles that they can only cast out a certain demon by "prayer and fasting." If Christ must fast, how is it possible that one who bears His name, a Christian, does not need to?

Perhaps most important, and most overlooked, is the fact that when we fast God blesses us. Fasting is not necessarily easy, but we are taught that this life is a struggle, and in our struggles we will be saved. We are athletes for God (this is where the word *asceticism* comes from), and when we eat at God's training table God blesses us, makes us healthier, and increases our spiritual capabilities.

Many people who do hold to the fast in their homes feel uncomfortable following the fast in public, or when entertaining guests. The Nativity fast is probably the most difficult fasting period of the year, as we are surrounded by friends and relatives holding Christmas parties and dinners, and it sometimes becomes difficult or uncomfortable not to not partake of what we are offered.

We should remember, however, that there are many people in our society who do not eat meat or milk products for philosophical reasons. They are called vegetarians if they do not eat meat, and vegans if they do not eat any animal products—milk, eggs, or fish. I notice that in general people who follow such diets, as well as pious Jews, Hindus and Moslems who hold strictly to their religious dietary laws are treated with great respect by friends, colleagues, and strangers. We Orthodox should not be afraid of following our own religious practice for fear of being thought of as "religious cranks."

Bearing in mind that there is both a "spirit" as well as a "letter" to the law, besides fasting from food we might also limit our entertainment. When fasting it is beneficial to limit time spent in front of the television, the movie screen or listening to music, and replace these amusements with reading spiritually edifying books, listening to recorded spiritual talks or lectures, etc. As it is much of what is shown on television nowadays (even in the afternoon) would have been censured as pornographic 40 or 50 years ago. Just as we are careful about what we put into our mouth when fasting we should be careful about what we feed our brain through our eyes and ears.

If you do not follow the fasting rules of the Church it is never too late to begin. If your not sure what to do or how to do it ask a spiritual father or pious layperson who themselves follow the fast (it is not wise to ask advice from people who have no experience of what they are talking about) how you might start. Even children can and should learn to fast from an early age. Delicious and nutritious meals do not necessarily need to include meat or animal products, and the example of Daniel and the three children in Babylon, as well as the counsel of doctors and nutritionists show us that we can easily follow the fasts of the Church without compromising our health.

Let us do our best to make our homes not only houses of prayer, but houses of fasting as well. And then let us see how God will bless us and strengthen us, both individually and as a Church. ■

Racing for Paradise

"Do you not know that those who run in a race all run, but one receives the prize? . . . And everyone who competes for the prize is temperate in all things. Now they do it to obtain a perishable crown, but we for an imperishable crown. Therefore I run thus: not with uncertainty. . . . But I discipline my body and bring it into subjection, lest, when I have preached to others, I myself should become disqualified" (1 Cor. 9:24–27).

He was taller than I, and walked in a loose-jointed sort of way. We were sitting on the grass stretching before the race. He came over and sat next to us.

After getting acquainted I asked, "So, how long have you been running?"

"A few months," he replied.

"How do you think you will do?"

"I think I have a good chance of winning," he said confidently.

I have seen stranger things happen, but the goal of someone who has been training for only a few months is usually just to finish comfortably. I knew some of the runners there that day—they were well-trained and fast. We talked a bit more about our training and expected finishing times, finished our warm-ups, and were off.

After completing the race I did my warm-down run, and was stretching when I saw him cross the finish line. He was a bit shaky, breathing hard, clearly having difficulty.

His disappointing performance was due to three simple mistakes. He trusted his feelings; he did not conform his training to an objective standard (a stop-watch or mile-post); and he was not properly prepared.

These same mistakes are often made by Orthodox Christians in their spiritual life.

We feel good about ourselves! "Of course, I am not perfect, but I go to Church. . . . not as much as I should, but I am so busy. . ., and anyway, I am better than most of the people I know who do not go to Church at all! And I am not like those hypocrites who go to Church every Sunday just for show. . . ."

Rather than look honestly at myself, consider my own weaknesses and attend to my own sins, how often do I just ignore them, smug and self-satisfied with the pleasant disposition or natural gifts God has given me? Such an approach would never get anyone to the Olympics, and it certainly will not get us into heaven. It is no coincidence that the Lenten prayer *par excellence*, the prayer of St. Ephraim, says *"Grant me to see my own sins, and not to judge my brother. . . ."*

This is not to say that we should not have a healthy sense of self-worth, as creatures made in God's image and unconditionally loved by Him. But if we think we can fulfill the teachings of Christ without ever experiencing a real sense of sinfulness or failure regarding our own personal ascetic struggle we are simply deluding ourselves.

We do not conform ourselves to an objective standard. "I know I'm not supposed to eat meat or dairy products during lent, but is not the main thing to be a good person? Just because I do not fast does not mean I am a bad person. I know lots of people who fast, but are simply intolerable!"

Christianity is not a "touchy-feely" religion. We have an objective standard of conduct to which we adhere. "Do not murder," "Honour your parents," "Do not steal," "Love your enemies," "Feed the hungry," "Pray," "Worship," "Read the Scriptures," "Confine sexual activity to a monogamous, heterosexual, loving marriage which has been blessed in Church." Christianity is a faith of commitment and sacrifice. Trying to meet the standard set for us by Christ and the Church is a difficult struggle.

Yet how often we see people trying to "lower the bar." People who want to be excused (e.g., "it is OK to eat steak on Friday night because the liturgical day begins at sundown so it is really Saturday") rather than be forgiven ("forgive me, I sinned by breaking the fast"). Using the metaphor of spiritual life as a race, the result of living a

"Christian life" according to personal subjective rather than biblical objective standards is exactly what happened to my friend in the race. We "crash and burn."

We are not properly prepared. Certain people argue that self-renunciation, abstinence in food, reading scripture instead of watching TV, are not that important. If we lived in an age where temptation was minimal this hypothesis might merit consideration. But in fact we live in a society where temptation presents itself on virtually every screen, page or billboard we see and every song or conversation we hear. For some of us fighting the temptation to sin is more difficult than running a marathon. And how do we train to fight temptation? By asceticism—prayer, fasting, almsgiving. The word asceticism means "exercise." Strengthening our will or self-control is just like strengthening our body. It takes exercise. This is what Lent and Christian discipline are all about.

There is only one difference between a spiritual race and a physical one. Only one runner wins an earthly race. Everyone can be a winner in the race for paradise.

"Do you not know that those who run in a race all run, but one receives the prize? Run in such a way that you may obtain it" (1Cor. 9:24). ■

Preparing for the Liturgy

Anyone who has ever taken a test—in school, for a driver's license, to get a job—knows the importance of proper preparation. Everything is easier and better when we are prepared for it. As the English saying goes, "well begun is half done." We take great care preparing for school, work, recreational activities, a concert, or a sporting event. How much more important is it, then, to attend Church services in a proper state of preparation?

Our preparation for Divine services consists of both spiritual and physical preparation, but it is important to emphasize the fact that Orthodox Christianity sees no dualism in our human nature. God has given us both a body and a soul, and everything we do to prepare for our worship and our participation in the sacramental life of the Church must be seen in this light. We must never believe that anything we do is "only physical" or "only spiritual," for indeed, both these aspects of our nature interpenetrate each other, and so the way we dress really can be as important as how we pray.

The atmosphere at home before we leave for Church. Whether we have a house full of children or live alone this is one of the most important aspects of our preparation. On the day when we will be attending Church services we must make sure that an atmosphere of peace and quiet expectation is maintained. All the hustle and bustle associated with our preparations for school and work, all the last minute searching for the proper clothes, etc. should be avoided. Orthodox Christians traditionally attend the vespers or vigil service the evening before a Liturgy, and maintain a quiet and pious atmosphere throughout the evening and night.

In our circumstances this "anticipatory" preparation might consist of preparing our clothes for Church the evening before so there is no need to do last minute searching; reading and reflecting on the scripture passages appointed for the Liturgy; reading a spiritually edifying book; not watching TV or listening to music (except perhaps ecclesiastical music); not listening to the news on the radio ("let us lay aside all earthly cares"); avoiding unnecessary conversation; and especially not doing or saying anything which will deflect either our own attention or the attention of those around us from the thought of what we are called upon to do in Church—to participate in the life of heaven.

How should we dress for Church? When we attend a Divine Service in the Church, we attend an extraordinary event in an extraordinary place. As we would make sure to be properly dressed if we were attending a formal dinner, going to a nice restaurant, having an important business meeting or being introduced to a person of great distinction, just as we "dress for success" in our worldly lives, we should take care to see that we are properly dressed when going to Church, for in the Holy Services we meet God Himself. What, then, are the generally accepted guidelines for proper dress in Church?

For men. While short pants are permissible for young boys, men should be in long pants, with a proper shirt on. Very informal clothing, such as T-shirts (especially if they have slogans, advertisements, or graphics on them), jeans should be avoided if at all possible. Tank tops, or any other type of shirt which does not cover the shoulders should never be worn. Men should never wear a hat, neither in the Church itself nor in the Church hall (As far as I know it is still considered bad manners for a man to wear a hat indoors anywhere at any time except for religious reasons).

For women. Women traditionally wear a skirt which extends to below the knee, a blouse which covers the shoulders, and some type of head-covering. It is interesting to note that only women and certain clergy are permitted to have their heads covered in Church—this is a sign of the special grace given them by God. The traditional head-covering is a scarf, although in the new world hats are sometimes worn. Short skirts or short pants as well as blouses or shirts which do not cover the shoulders or are excessively revealing should be avoided at all times.

Regarding cosmetics we should have the same approach as towards our dress, i.e., to be simple and not ostentatious. While we all like to look nice, we remember that God sees us as we truly are, and we should not be overly concerned with how we look to others, because true beauty is the beauty of a loving heart and soul. One important caveat is that lipstick should not be worn, and if for some reason a woman is wearing lipstick she should wipe it off before approaching to kiss the cross or an icon, and especially before approaching for Holy Communion. Lipstick, as we all know, is difficult to clean from icons, crosses and other objects, and in the case of wood can actually leave a permanent stain. A great Orthodox saint and wonderworker of the 20th century, St. John of Shanghai and San Francisco, would actually lift the cross high over his head if a woman wearing lipstick approached to kiss it, so that it was physically impossible for her to do so!

For everyone. Our clothes should be clean, neat and simple. We should not wear clothes that will draw undue attention either to us or to the clothes themselves, for our attention in Church should be drawn to God.

Having said this, we must also remember that there are many, many people in our community who have never been taught how to dress appropriately for Church or for other occasions and functions. If anyone attends services dressed in an inappropriate manner (and in this day and age there are many, many people who have no idea what the phrase "proper dress" means) we should not judge them, nor give them the "hairy eyeball" and make them feel uncomfortable so that they never wish to return to the Church. Instead we should do our best to help them, lovingly and respectfully, to become acquainted with why and how we dress, cross ourselves, and behave in church, because all of these things are intimately involved with our Faith.

What we should (and should not) eat. In general, the answer to this question is very simple. We should not eat anything. It is generally accepted that in the early Church everyone present at the Liturgy approached for Holy Communion unless there was a good reason for them not to (e.g., if they were doing penance for a grave sin, or maybe were not properly prepared), and prior to receiving Holy Communion we are not permitted to eat or drink anything from the preceding evening (at least from midnight), the so-called Eucharistic fast. It is beneficial to maintain this same practice whenever we attend the Divine Liturgy, whether we are communing or not.

Why is this so? The remnants of the Eucharistic breads, called the *Antidoron* (which means "instead of the gift"), are given out to those who do not commune at the Liturgy and so, at least theoretically, everyone present at the Liturgy should partake either of the Eucharist or the antidoron. Even though it is inconceivable for many Orthodox to imagine everyone, or even most of those present in Church, approaching for Holy Communion at a single Liturgy, we are exhorted to approach for antidoron just as we do for Holy Communion—on an empty stomach. Our Christian tradition gives us other examples of this as well—the faithful, for instance, are instructed that Holy Water (especially after the Great Hallowing of Waters on the Theophany) is to be taken on an empty stomach.

This Eucharistic or Liturgical fast does not, of course, pertain to medicines or foods which are necessary for our health. If, for example, a person is diabetic, they often must have specific foods at specific times to control this disease. If a person must take medication for a heart condition or any other illness they are permitted to do so. Health is a gift of God, and must be respected. But it is understood that in such circumstances the faithful will eat only what is absolutely necessary, abstaining from that which is unnecessary, and have the blessing of their spiritual father to do so.

The Eucharistic fast has been likened to a "fast of anticipation," which serves the purpose of increasing our attention at the Liturgy. As we all know, it is easier to think on an empty stomach, and a full stomach makes us sleepy. This fast also teaches us in a very physical, concrete way that a Sunday or Holy day is different. We read in the 50th Psalm that *". . . a sacrifice unto God is a broken spirit. . . ."* Giving up that first cup of coffee in the morning can also be a truly meaningful sacrifice! Making fasting a part of our preparation will bring great benefits to our spiritual life, not the least of which will be increased participation in the sacramental life of the Church.

Prayer & Scripture reading. Finally we come to one of the most generally practiced ways of preparing ourselves—prayer and reading of Holy Scripture. It is commonly accepted that every member of the faithful have a specific rule of prayer, which they follow daily. This rule of prayer should be discussed with and blessed by one's spiritual father, and performed faithfully. If this is done, then the only thing necessary to add are the specific prayers indicated when approaching for Holy Communion. These consist of the canon, psalms and prayers before Holy Communion, and the prayers after Holy Communion. Where a rule of prayer is not followed we should contact our priest or a spiritual father for advice on how we might begin.

It is commonly accepted that every member of the Church will regularly and diligently read the Holy Scriptures. When we will be attending Liturgy we should read and meditate upon the passages of the day (which can be done either the night before or the morning of the Liturgy), so that we might receive ultimate benefit from our attendance and more deeply comprehend the meaning of the festal or Sunday Liturgy. Where possible it is very beneficial for the entire family to be together as the passages for the day are read aloud, and even to discuss them in the car on the way to Church. Thank God that there are many excellent resources to make this easy—any good Church calendar, The Bible and Fathers for Orthodox by Johanna Manley; and The Orthodox Study Bible by Conciliar Press are three that come immediately to mind.

In closing, it is perhaps worthwhile to emphasize that it is not only what something is, but also what it means that is often important. A dried rose on an old woman's mantle, for example, might be just a dried rose to anyone else, but for the woman herself it might be the last rose her husband gave her before he died, and so has very great meaning to her. Our preparation for Liturgy helps us put meaning into an act which some (sad to say) find burdensome or tiring. But for those properly prepared and properly disposed to it the Liturgy can a joyful event, more meaningful than a dried rose on a mantelpiece, and a true manifestation of the wisdom, love, and power of God. ■

Vespers

One of the things which virtually all heterodox Christian denominations have lost, but our Orthodox Church still possesses, is the "liturgy of the hours." This is the cycle of services identified with the different hours of the day or night. Besides the Divine Liturgy our service books contain eight other liturgical services: Vespers; the After-supper service (Compline); the Midnight Office; Orthros (Matins); and the First, Third, Sixth, and Ninth hours.

These other services were universally known throughout the undivided Christian Church of the first millennium, and still remain in an abbreviated form within the Roman Catholic and Anglican traditions. Within the universal Orthodox Church they continue to be served daily in monasteries and large parish churches which possess the required human and clerical resources.

Due to the fact that most parishes do not have the requisite readers, cantors and clergy to perform all of these services, the custom of serving at least the main services of the liturgical day—Vespers and Orthros—has become common in parish life. According to the Greek tradition the main service apart from and in preparation for the Divine Liturgy is the morning service—Orthros (Matins). In the Slavic tradition it is generally the evening service, called Vespers.

What is Vespers? Vespers is a worship service, usually begun between 5:00 and 7:00 P.M., associated since ancient times with the setting of the sun and the lighting of the lamps.

In the book of Genesis God creates first night, and then day: "...the evening and the morning were the first day" (Gen. 1:5). We Orthodox follow this biblical paradigm and count the liturgical day from sundown. Vespers, then, is the first service of the liturgical day. Vespers, as almost all our liturgical prayer, is a direct outgrowth as well as the fulfillment of the liturgical worship we see described in the

Old Testament as given by God to the Israelites and practiced in the Temple in Jerusalem.

Vespers is composed of Psalms, hymns, poetic and didactic compositions, and prayers appropriate to the time of day and the feast(s) which are being celebrated. It begins with the opening prayers, followed by the reading or singing of Psalm 103 and the Litany of peace. After the litany a kathisma (a selection of psalms) is usually read, although in parish usage this is often abbreviated or omitted.

Following the kathisma Psalm 140—"*Lord I have cried unto Thee, hearken unto me. . . . Let my prayer arise like incense before Thee, the lifting of my hands like the evening sacrifice. . . .*"—is chanted, followed by Psalms 141, 129 and 116. While the chanting takes place the priest or deacon censes the entire temple and the lamps are lit. The first set of poetic and didactic (educational) verses (called *stychyry*) are then chanted. This section is always completed by the singing of a Theotokion (hymn to the Mother of God), and on Saturday evening as well as the eve of feasts the clergy make an entrance with the censer or Gospel.

"O Tranquil Light," an ancient hymn to Christ as the True Light is then sung, followed by the prokeimen (responsorial psalm). On great feasts Old Testament readings are appointed, followed by the litany of fervent supplication, "*Vouchsafe, O Lord. . . .*" (the evening prayer), the "askings" (litany of supplication) and the head-bowing prayer.

On the eve of a feast day the Litia, a procession with a special litany for the Church and civil authorities, the nation, her people and all the faithful, may be appointed here. The aposticha, a second set of poetic verses are sung at this point, followed by the Song of Simeon (Lk. 2:29) and the trisagion prayers. The troparia (hymns of the day) are then sung, followed by the dismissal.

According to the Byzantine tradition Vespers is served by itself in the evening, and will last from 45 to 70 minutes, depending on the feast being celebrated and the manner in which the service is sung. In the Russian tradition, as well as in many monasteries, it is often combined with Orthros (the morning service) and the first hour into a longer service called the "All-night Vigil." The vigil can take anywhere from three to five hours to serve in full.

Vespers was an integral part of the religious life of our forebears. Nowadays, sadly, it is rare to find a parish where vespers is regularly celebrated. Where it is celebrated it is common to hear the priest lament: "I serve Vespers every Saturday, but I am lucky if I have two or three people in Church. It is usually only me and the cantor."

One reason this happens is that Vespers can be an extremely boring and ugly service if it is not done well. There is nothing less edifying than a priest and cantor mumbling back and forth unintelligibly in a foreign language and calling it Vespers. One often gets the impression they are trying to get to the end of the service as quickly as possible so that they can get on with "important and interesting" things. If this is the attitude of those leading the service why would anyone else want to attend?

For Vespers to be successfully integrated into the life of the parish it is necessary for the service to be peaceful, edifying, and beautiful. The words must be clearly sung, the melodies should be simple, and the participation of the faithful must be actively encouraged.

But is not it enough to attend Liturgy? Why should I attend Vespers, too? There are two main reasons: first of all, to enhance and enrich my own spiritual life; and secondly, to enhance the spirituality of my parish.

If I listen to the verses and hymns of the day I will learn a lot about my faith (provided, obviously, that they are sung in a language I can understand). We, likewise receive God's grace and blessings for the sacrifices, honor and glory we offer Him—the more we honor Him, the greater the blessings and grace we receive. And if we are in Church, and not in front of the TV, or computer, or on the telephone, we will spend less time being influenced by worldly, questionable, and sometimes downright evil enticements.

Christians are supposed to be people of prayer. Prayers offered by more people, more often, are stronger. And we cannot forget that the parish, like any group, is only as strong as its members. The stronger the individual parishioners are in their own spiritual life, the stronger the parish will be.

When Vespers becomes a regular (and this means <u>every</u> Saturday and <u>every</u> great feast day) and well-attended part of the parish schedule we will see other benefits as well. It is a good evangelical tool in that it is an excellent service for enquirers to attend. Those interested in Orthodoxy will usually be attending their own church on Sunday morning, or else be sleeping in. But a service on Saturday in the early evening is accessible to all. In addition, it is a lot shorter than a full Liturgy, the priest is usually not pressed with all kinds of commitments afterwards and so has time to sit down and converse with enquirers, and since it is not a Eucharistic service the issues regarding the sacramental participation of non-Orthodox are absent.

"Father, I cannot attend Liturgy because I have to work." How often priests hear these words! Vespers offers everyone an option when their work or school schedules conflict with liturgy. We as Orthodox do not do "the mass on Saturday night" thing like the Catholics, and Vespers should not be seen as a substitute for the Liturgy, but if I absolutely cannot attend liturgy in the morning (especially on week-days) Vespers gives me an opportunity to liturgically celebrate the holy days with the Church.

On top of all these benefits is the fact that vespers is a school for cantors. One of the greatest shortages we face is not a shortage of priests, but a shortage of trained cantors. Attending and singing Vespers every week gives us the opportunity to learn the different liturgical tones and chants, and to practice our liturgical singing in a setting which is a lot more informal and "forgiving" than the Sunday Eucharistic Liturgy.

It has been noted that how we worship on Sunday morning depends very much on how we prepare on Saturday night. Going out on Saturday evening to "sow your wild oats," and then coming to Church on Sunday to pray for a crop failure is not, perhaps, the best way of approaching worship!

If we wish to have a healthy parish, a grace-filled Church, and a rich Christian life, we could do worse than to make attendance at Vespers a priority. ■

THE HOLY MYSTERIES

Get Married? Why Bother?

One of the most joyful events in life is marriage. The beauty of the service, the elegance of the clothes and gowns, the love of family and friends, and the presence of God make each wedding a unique and memorable event. Yet many people nowadays do not bother getting married. Many people who consider themselves good Christians are, in fact, dead set against this sacrament. Does marriage really make a difference in a relationship?

Our Church teaches us that conjugal love between a man and a woman is a holy thing, and is properly manifested and guarded within the bonds of marriage. The Church understands marriage to be an honorable state, a consecrated state, and for this reason treats it as a Holy Mystery.

The central symbol of the marriage is the crowning of the bride and groom. The ring is a sign of betrothal, not marriage, and vows are not part of the Orthodox marriage service. It is in the crowning, symbolic of the martyrdom of the couple, symbolic of the fact that they are called to give their lives for each other, that the sacramental act is solemnized. The Roman Catholic and Protestant theologies of marriage differ from that of the Orthodox. Until the Roman Church left Orthodoxy the theology of marriage, like the faith, was shared in both East and West. In the 13th century the Roman Church introduced wedding vows, which changed the essential understanding of the sacrament of marriage from an act performed by God to one "exchanged" by the bride and groom. When the various protestant groups broke off from the Roman Church during the reformation they took with them this "man-centered" understanding of marriage, and emptied it of its sacramental meaning as well.

When we speak of Christian marriage we refer specifically to the Orthodox service of crowning. While not daring to judge Catholics or Protestants (many of whom individually often have much stronger marriages than particular Orthodox couples) we must plainly state that we understand the fullness of sacramental marriage (as well as the fullness of the Christian faith) to be present in Orthodoxy. Most of our young people in North America marry non-Orthodox spouses. The Church does not recognize "mixed marriages," and so this creates a problem. If an Orthodox Christian wishes to marry a person who has not been baptized this person must be baptized before any Church wedding is permitted. In North America most Orthodox Churches will perform the marriage "by economia" if one of the bridal pair is Orthodox and the other has been baptized with water in the name of the Holy Trinity. Due to the fact that many protestant sects do not practice a proper form of baptism (sprinkling rather than immersion) and do not use a Trinitarian formula priests are often put into uncomfortable situations, especially when the Orthodox party (or their parents) do not understand what baptism is, what it means, or what it is for. In cases where there is any doubt about a person's baptism they should be baptized, not only so a wedding might take place, but more importantly for the eternal salvation of the person involved.

When a couple of two different faiths decides to marry one of the big problems is often "whose Church?" This is a delicate matter. "He who does not have the Church for their mother cannot have God for their Father," says the ancient Christian proverb. Being a faithful member of the Orthodox Church means having recourse to her for all our spiritual needs. She therefore insists that her children be married in the Orthodox Church.

We should not see this requirement of our faith as coercion. We take the religious beliefs of other Christians seriously, often much more seriously than they do themselves. In the given instance we would make the point that no other Christian bodies (with the exception of Eastern-rite Roman Catholics) crown the marriage. The Orthodox marriage is recognized by all other Christian churches. For these reasons we would propose that there is no need for anyone on purely religious grounds to be married outside the Orthodox Church.

Orthodox Christians who willfully marry outside the Church excommunicate themselves. According to the canons they are not permitted to approach for any of the Holy Mysteries—confession and communion first among them. This may seem extreme to some, but given the fact that Holy Communion is our central sacramental act as baptized Christians, it reminds us of the fact that the life of the Church must be taken as a whole—it is not a "pick and choose" affair. When we deny one of the Holy Mysteries, we deny them all.

Why is Church so sticky about this? Is not marriage a private affair? Is not it between me and my spouse? Why is the Church so judgmental?

The fact of the matter is that the Church is not judgmental at all. Sexual immorality is probably one of the most destructive factors in social and societal life. Marriage serves a very important function in regulating sexual activity. In addition, it is important to remember that married life is consecrated life. It would be scandalous for an un-ordained layperson to put on the priest's vestments and serve the Liturgy. Acting like a husband, or wife, or parent without the sacramental grace of Christian marriage is no different.

We need God's help in everything—the more difficult the task, the more we need it. Having a successful marriage is hard work. We may get it done on our own, but if we really do believe in God why would we purposely exclude Him from the equation?

I am sure we have all heard many different reasons and excuses why people do not marry: "a marriage license is just a piece of paper." That is true. So is the deed to your house, your passport, or your driver's license. So be consistent. Either accept that the marriage license represents an important reality just like those other documents do, or try to live without them, too.

"We will get married eventually." Good, but why not now?

"We do not have the money to get married now." This particular statement was made to me by a couple who had just bought a house one month earlier. They had the money for a $150,000 house, but not for a marriage ceremony!

The worst reason people do not get married in Church is probably selfishness. It is a case of the relationship being about Me, or about Us, but not about God. This attitude often goes hand-in-hand with a lack of faith and trust in God for sure, and often in the partner as well.

Sometimes couples do not marry for economic reasons. Older couples, for example, might have pension issues. A woman who is receiving her reposed husband's pension may lose it if she gets married, and the pension of her husband-to-be is not enough for them to live on. These are delicate matters, best dealt with on an individual basis. In general, however, even if it is a quiet, church-only service, the couple should be crowned. No one is too old, no one is too poor. The true love of senior citizens is no different than the true love of teenagers. When they cohabit without marriage, however, it is much worse. They should know better. They should give a good example to younger people, especially if they claim to belong to the Church.

People who have not been married in the Church often are embarrassed about regularizing the marriage. There is nothing more beautiful than two people standing before God, asking Him to be an integral part of their relationship. Any priest worth his salt (and there are such priests) will do his best to accommodate anyone who wishes to draw nearer to God in this way. For one couple it might be a strictly private affair between them and the priest. For another it might be a full-blown wedding. The main thing is that the relationship is sacramentally offered to God, that He might bless it, and return it to us, better and more perfect.

Preparing young people for marriage from an early age—teaching them sacramental theology as well as the theological anthropology and the real "sex education" of the Church—is an important way of dealing with this problem. The role of marriage preparation courses for those preparing to be wed is also important. Arranging seminars, retreats, and other gatherings for married couples is the third link in this chain, the one which most often is missing.

In this day and age when marriage is being attacked philosophically, politically, economically and socially, we must do our best to remind society as a whole and our young people in particular that marriage is a sacred and sanctifying state, that it opens for us the doors to participation in God's creative activity, and that for most of us it will be the most important relationship of our life—not apart from our relationship with God, but in conjunction with it. ∎

Intercommunion

Priests are occasionally asked: "Father, my friend (or relative) is not Orthodox, but they would like to receive Holy Communion in our Church. Are they allowed?" Conversely, it often happens that our faithful who attend weddings or funerals in churches of other denominations, or are in hospitals or nursing homes, are offered Holy Communion by the clergy or Eucharistic ministers of heterodox denominations. The priest often finds out about this afterwards, when during conversation the faithful involved say "and by the way, father, I was given communion by a Catholic—is it all right?

Simply saying "no" to either question often makes the priest appear to be "intolerant" or uncharitable. But the fact of the matter is that we should not commune in other churches, nor is it permitted to commune non-Orthodox in our Church. Why?

In order to understand who may and who may not approach for the Holy Mystery of the Eucharist we must first understand what the Eucharist is. We know that the Church has always believed and taught that the consecrated bread and wine truly become the Most Holy Body and Blood of Our Lord, Jesus Christ. This Eucharist is present with us, but it is also a "remembrance" of the past (the Mystical Supper, our Lord's sacrifice on Golgotha), and somehow also it exists above all time—eternally. It is at the same time worldly and heavenly—temporal and eternal. It is not a symbol of our Lord, it is our Lord; It is not only a symbol of a historical act, it is God in heaven present among and within us.

The Eucharist, also known from Apostolic times as the "breaking of the bread," has been the defining act of every Christian in every age. As Jesus said, *"Whoever eats My flesh and drinks my blood has eternal life"* (John 6:54). Even though most Orthodox Christians do not commune at every Liturgy, we still serve the Liturgy on all Sundays and Holy days. Why serve a Liturgy, and not a moleben or paraklisis? We do this because the Liturgy—the Eucharist—is that which constitutes the Church. As the Christians martyred in 303 A.D. in Abilinitina, North Africa explained when asked by their tormenters why they continued to attend Sunday Liturgy knowing full well that the authorities were waiting to arrest them: *"Without the Sunday Eucharist we do not exist."*

Likewise, as we know, the Eucharist is the "mystery of faith" *par excellence.* In every other Holy Mystery the properties of the physical manifestation of the mystery remain the same—blessed water or oil is blessed, but it is still water or oil. In the Eucharist we are faced with the fact that the bread and the wine are changed into God's Body and Blood. We can only understand this through the eyes of faith, and historically it has been only those who hold the faith of the Church who are permitted to partake of the Holy Mysteries, especially of the Eucharist.

Confession of and taking full responsibility for the true, Apostolic, Orthodox Christian Faith, and membership in the Church have always been the requirements for receiving Holy Communion. Likewise, when one of the faithful transgressed God's law (by committing a grave sin such as murder, adultery, preaching heresy, or denying the faith) the gravest consequence has always been excommunication—which literally means the denial of Holy Communion. If anyone is not a member in good standing of the Church (spiritually and morally) or does not hold the Orthodox Faith they are not permitted to approach the chalice.

So we see that the Holy Mystery of the Eucharist has, like the Holy Cross, both a vertical and a horizontal dimension—vertically, it is our union with God, and horizontally, it is our union with the Church (both now and throughout all ages). Those who do not hold the True Faith with regards to the Eucharist (the protestant denominations for example, who teach that the bread and wine only symbolize Christ's body and blood, and therefore cannot be understood as uniting us to God) are not permitted to approach because their faith is lacking, and those who are not united to the Orthodox Church (the Catholics, for example, who while still acknowledging that the Eucharist is truly Jesus' Body and Blood differ in their understanding of what constitutes the Church) are forbidden because we do not have unity with them in the Body of Christ, the Church.

Lest anyone think that the Orthodox Church is intolerant or judgmental towards others in this matter, it must be underlined that not every Orthodox Christian is permitted to approach the Holy Chalice. Orthodox who have committed grave sins (murder, sex outside of the marriage bond, apostasy from the faith, etc.), and those who have broken the discipline of the Church (by contracting a marriage outside of the Church, for example) are forbidden to approach for Holy Communion until such time as they have truly repented of their sin, approached for Holy Confession, and done what is necessary or possible to right the wrong they have committed. Why is this so? Because the Eucharist is the Most Holy Mystery, it is Christ Himself, and we dare not adopt a lighthearted attitude towards it. Remember that the first thing the priest or deacon says when calling us to the Cup is *"With fear of God. . . ."*

So in answering this question of whether non-Orthodox are permitted to Holy Communion it is important to remember that the opportunity to approach for the Eucharist is a privilege, not a right. This applies to Orthodox as well as non-Orthodox, and is based on our Faith, Church membership and Christian life. Likewise, the fact that non-Orthodox are not permitted to the Cup is in no way to be construed as a judgment of their souls—the only ones we should ever be judging are ourselves, and our own sins. But the fact is that there has never been communion in the Holy Mysteries where communion in the same faith did not exist first, not for the Apostles, not for the Saints, and not for us. And understanding this, for all of us who truly desire that denominationalism and sectarianism within Christianity will cease and we will truly have the "One Church" which Our Lord desires, the words which we pray at every Liturgy take on added meaning—*"Having asked for unity of the Faith, and communion in the Holy Spirit, let us commend ourselves, and one another, and our whole life unto Christ our Lord."* ■

Preparing for Confession

One of the most efficacious of the Holy Mysteries given us by Our Lord is the Holy Mystery of Confession. In the Gospel read on Antipascha (St. Thomas Sunday) we hear the Risen Christ say to the Apostles *"Whosoever sins you forgive they are forgiven, and whosoever sins you retain they are retained."* In the absolution prayer read over the earthly remains of an Orthodox Christian at their funeral we repeat these words, and underline that this grace of binding and loosing from sins has been passed down from the apostles to our very day by the act of ordination. So in answering the question "what is Holy Confession" we can say that it is our participation in the act of God's forgiveness of our sins by the grace of the Holy Spirit given to the apostles by Christ.

Confession has essentially two main goals—one is the cleansing and forgiveness of sin, and the second is preparation for Holy Communion. When we consider the fact that the reason Jesus was born, the reason that God became incarnate, took on flesh, suffered, died, was raised from the dead and ascended into heaven for our sakes was and is for the forgiveness of sins, we see that our attitude toward this great mystery should be properly respectful. The entire life of the Church exists for the forgiveness of sin—if we do not need forgiveness of sins there is really no need for any of the Holy Mysteries. If it is true that you only "get out of something what you put into it," then perhaps confession is worth a proper preparation.

In preparing for confession the most important and most widely known practices are prayer and fasting. We pray to God to help us make a good confession, we should read the canon of repentance in preparation for confession, and we fast in an appropriate manner. Besides the Eucharistic fast we should always strictly observe the Wednesday and Friday fasts the week before receiving Holy Communion, and for those who receive Communion infrequently (three or four times a year or less) it is beneficial to abstain from all meat and dairy products for the entire week before communing.

We pray in the Lord's prayer: *". . . and forgive us our trespasses as we forgive those who trespass against us. . . ."* Approaching God to ask forgiveness of our sins without having asked forgiveness of those we have offended here on earth is not proper. Jesus teaches us that if we have anything against anyone when we are bringing our gift to the altar we should leave our gift, make peace with our brother or sister, and then return to offer our gift to God. Practically speaking, before we even consider approaching for sacramental confession we should consider the state of our life, consider if there is anyone against whom we have sinned, or who might have something against us. If this is so, then we should make peace with them in our heart, and if possible even personally. We must keep in mind, however, that if such an act were to be misconstrued by other people it could contribute to an even worse situation, and so the manner of and degree to which we will openly ask forgiveness of others is probably as different as each one of us. That we must have peace and no ill will against anyone in our heart is, however, absolutely necessary.

The tradition of asking forgiveness of others before confession is manifested in a beautiful custom still followed in certain places. We might occasionally see (or have seen) a person either before confession or before communion stand in the middle of the temple and bow (usually to the ground) to the faithful on either side of the Church. This gesture says: *"I have sinned against God and against you, my brothers and sisters. Forgive me and pray for me."* This is an excellent custom to be retained where it still exists, and to introduce back into parish life where it has died out.

For all of us, but especially for those who have never been properly prepared to understand the meaning and purpose of Holy Confession one of the most beneficial things we can do in preparation for confession is to read books about this Holy Mystery. In addition to a good prayer book which contains the prayers in preparation for confession and communion there are several excellent texts which are readily available: If we confess our sins by Fr. Thomas Hopko, a "how to" book of preparation and prayers for adults; We return to God by

Fr. Constance Tarasar, the same type of book, but for children and youth; The Forgotten Medicine by Archimandrite Seraphim Aleksiev, a beautiful book explaining the spiritual meaning of Holy Confession; and Repentance and Confession by Fr. John Chryssavgis which contains both an explanation of and many quotes from the Holy Fathers on repentance and confession. The section of the book These are the Sacraments by Fr. Anthony Coniaris which deals with Confession is also very good.

When should we approach for Holy Confession? The short answer is anytime! In some Churches the practice is to approach for Holy Confession immediately before the Liturgy begins. This practice, however, is not ideal. The priest is under a strict time constraint, and if there are many people approaching it can interfere with his preparation for the Liturgy. Approaching on Saturday either before or after vespers is better, as this gives both the priest and us the opportunity to approach this great mystery in a solemn and unhurried manner.

It is worth remembering that in any traditional Christian country Saturday night was not a time to go out drinking, to banquets, or to parties—it was the time to prepare for Sunday Liturgy. It was a time of quiet and joyful expectation, usually spent quietly with family. Visiting, parties, and other festivities were held on Sunday, after Liturgy. Even though many parishes do not serve vespers or the vigil on Saturday evening (an unfortunate and unhealthy situation) it is still important to pass this evening in a pious manner, especially if we will be approaching for Holy Communion the next day. We remember that just as dancing, loud music and parties are forbidden during Lent (since our concentration should be on our spiritual preparation for the feast of the Resurrection) the fasting we do in preparation for receiving Holy Communion at any time of the year is no different.

One of the most frequently asked questions by those who are preparing for confession for the first time is "what do I say"? Holy Confession is undoubtedly the most "free form" of all the Mysteries. The various Books of Needs give a specific, yet different, order for the service, (depending on the Church tradition) which is followed to a greater or lesser degree depending on the time, age, state and situation of the penitent and the priest. Generally speaking there are introductory prayers, prayers for a good confession, and an admonition to the penitent which are read by the priest; following this there is the confession of sins by the penitent, during which the priest may or may not ask questions of them; following this the priest will generally give an exhortation or perhaps give some advice on how to better live the Christian life; and then he will generally read the prayer of absolution. There really is no "formula" for the penitent to recite—as long as they have done a proper examination of their conscience in advance and have prayed for God's guidance they will know what to say when the time comes. As long as there is repentance in our hearts our words will always be correct.

Another frequently asked question is "I can confess to God in my heart—after all, God sees and knows all. Why do I have to confess to a priest?" Two points have to be made. First of all, we do not believe that confession is either a public or a private matter—public and private confession are both important and necessary. Every one of us should be privately confessing our sins to God every day, as well as approaching for sacramental confession as often as possible. Secondly, we do not confess our sins to the priest—we confess them to God. The job of the priest is to represent the Church, and to speak the words of forgiveness on behalf of God. Technically speaking, a confession with no one else present, as well as a "confession" in which a penitent does not mention any sins are not confessions at all. A confession is the public acknowledgment of something (in this case sin). This is why public confession has always been practiced in the Christian Church.

Many of us have probably read about, or seen in television shows and movies the Roman Catholic manner of confession, and are aware of the fact that Catholics are often given "penances," usually a specific number of prayers to recite as a mark of their repentance. Is this a part of our tradition? Is the priest permitted to give us a "penance" after Holy Confession, and are we obliged to fulfill it in order for our sins to be forgiven? The short answer is yes, but this question has two aspects that require explanation—the grace of "binding and loosing," and the understanding of confession as a therapeutic mystery.

If the Apostles truly were given the grace to bind and loose sins, then there is no question that every sin revealed in confession might be retained, that is, not forgiven sacramentally. The reason for this is very simple—such a great gift, the gift of forgiveness of sins by God must not be treated in a hypocritical manner. A person who approaches confession with no contrition for their sins, with no repentance in their heart, is not looking for forgiveness, they are only looking to be "validated," along with their sinful lives, by the Church. Such a person would make both themselves and especially the priest and the Church hypocrites were they to approach for confession in such a mental and spiritual state. Another example might be a person who has committed a great sin, such as murder, but has not been found or perhaps even suspected for this crime. What happens if a priest hears this person's confession, and not being able to reveal this sin to any other living person (for the "seal of the confessional"—the total secrecy of anything said while the priest has the stole around his neck—is absolute) at the same time recognizes that he cannot simply say "that is OK, it does not matter" and read the absolution prayer over the person. In such circumstances a penitential act would be in order. In the first circumstance the priest might prescribe an act (perhaps something as simple as the penitent walking to the middle of the Church to bow to the faithful and ask their forgiveness as was outlined above) that will instill repentance in their heart; in the second instance, the priest might tell the penitent that they must first turn themselves in to the police or in some other way take responsibility for their crime before the absolution prayer will be read and they will be permitted to approach for Holy Communion. The principle involved is therapeutic. A "penance" is not a punishment for a sin, but a prescription for a healthy spiritual life. While the above examples are extreme and not in any way common, it might happen that a penitent has a particular sinful inclination which might be helped by reading a specific book or passage of the Gospel or by engaging in some type of volunteer work with the less fortunate. When such an act is prescribed by the priest in confession we must remember that it is for our benefit, and will help us in our spiritual growth and health. The exhortation read by the priest before the confession of sins according to the Slavic tradition says "beware, that having approached the

Doctor, you depart unhealed." The Doctor is Christ, and in approaching for confession, we approach for the healing of our souls.

Between the time of confession and Holy Communion, in addition to considering the magnitude of the grace of God given to us and trying to remain as much as possible in a state of sinlessness, we should read the prayers in preparation for Holy Communion. It is beneficial to read these beautiful prayers slowly, considering every sentence and every phrase. As we approach for Holy Communion we remember that we are partaking of Christ's sacrificial death and resurrection—and that in Holy Communion we receive the completion of the forgiveness we asked of God in Holy Confession. Following Communion we should joyfully read the prayers after Holy Communion, and spend the whole day in a joyful, spiritually peaceful manner.

Let us remember the words of Theodore of Mopsuestia, who writes: *"If we have committed a serious sin of any kind which implies rejection of God's will, we must abstain from Communion. But we must not allow ourselves to stay away indefinitely. No, indeed, we must rouse ourselves to repentance. We must not leave the healing of sins to themselves. God has given us the remedy of confession, according to the discipline of the Church. This is the treatment of sins that God has entrusted to the priests of the Church."* ■

Who are you?

"Who are you?" "I know your name, I know your family, but I do not know you."

The phone call I got about you was the one I dread. "Father, so and so has passed away, and the family wants to know when you can serve the funeral."

What am I supposed to do? I have been in this parish long enough to have seen and met anyone who has even the slightest connection with our community. I have never seen you in Church. I have never spoken with you. I have never noticed you at a memorial service, a wedding, a baptism, or a funeral. Where have you been? Were you a believer? If you were a believer, you certainly did not act like one. What I mean is that there has always been a clear set of expectations set before anyone who wishes to call themselves a Christian. Christians approach for Holy Confession and Holy Communion at least once a year, for example. You did not. Christians support the Church with their time, money, and talents. You did not. Christians attend Divine Services regularly. You, to my knowledge, and to the knowledge of everyone I have talked to, have not darkened the door of our church in years.

From what I have been told you were rather successful at what you did. You obviously spent lots of time learning career skills, spent lots of time working and making money. From your address I see that you certainly were well off financially. But even this confuses me, because our parish keeps records of everyone who donates even the smallest amount of money, and I have never seen your name there. You had money for the government. You had money for food. You had money for shelter, for vacations, for a cottage, for concerts, and for restaurants. Yet now that you are dead it is the Church, the same Church you did not support when you had the chance, that gets asked to bury you.

"But he was baptized here," they tell me. Sometimes I think the sectarians are right, and we should wait until people reach the age of reason so that they might consciously accept baptism, with all its consequences and responsibilities. The fact that you were baptized here simply underlines the fact that someone failed—perhaps your family, perhaps our community, perhaps you yourself—in your Christian upbringing and development. If you had not been baptized you (and your parents and godparents) would at least have an excuse for your conduct.

At times like this I just want to go on vacation, and let a substitute priest deal with things, because not knowing the situation at least he will not have qualms of conscience. Did you believe in God, or did you mock God? Were you positively disposed to the Church and Her teachings, or did you actively support social and moral teachings such as access to abortion which are anti-Christian? Not knowing these things, I do not know if it is proper to bury you. A Christian burial is for Christians. Were you? The Church always tries to give the benefit of the doubt, but we have to base that benefit on something. So far, I am drawing a blank.

What do I say to your family? They are distressed and heartbroken. All of us realize that death is just around the corner, that a weak heart, a drunk driver, or any of a myriad of other causes can snuff out our life even as we feel ourselves to be young, healthy, and in control of our destiny. Your sudden death, not having time to say even a simple "good-bye, I love you" has devastated them. I hope there were no unresolved conflicts, because in a case like this they usually make those left behind even more distraught, and sometimes such wounds never heal.

The one thing I can say for sure is that you do have a few devout family members, people who truly love God and serve Him in any way they can. While most of your friends and family would probably be only mildly upset if I did not bury you (I actually think most of them would be happier. A "rent-a-preacher" service would be shorter and more easily forgotten, and afterwards they wold be able to complain about how the priest was "unfair" or "judgmental" and feel justified in not having anything to do with the Church. Until they wanted a nice wedding. Or to baptize their child. Or died), it is these pious relatives who are foremost in my mind as I consider what to do.

As the saying goes, "God has children, but no grandchildren." It does not matter whether our parents or aunts or uncles are saintly, or priests, or bishops, or monastics, it is what we ourselves do with the time, talents and material wealth which God has given to us which will either open or lock the gates of Heaven for us. If we do not want to be saved even God Himself cannot force us (and God can do anything!).

The bottom line, you see, is that I do not feel comfortable making either you, or me, or the Church into a hypocrite. Jesus preached love, but He also preached truth and responsibility. He accepted the worst sinners who repented, but he condemned everyone (the "church people" first and foremost!) who were hypocritical. So you see, my problem is not that you were a sinner. I am a sinner too. My problem is that if you consciously chose not to have anything to do with the Church during your lifetime then burying you from the Church makes you into a hypocrite, which I do not want to do. If I decide to bury you for a stipend, or just in order not to "make waves" in the community, I am then a hypocrite. And if hypocritical priests bury hypocritical laymen it certainly makes the Church appear hypocritical, does it not?

"But the Church is full of hypocritical people," you might say. You are right, and again, I am one of them. I personally would rather deal with an honest agnostic than a nominal believer. But the very fact that someone is willing to give God the benefit of the doubt (if not real faith) by paying their parish membership, by being well disposed towards the Church, by showing up for the occasional religious or cultural or social gathering really does mean something. We are taught that when we take one step towards God, He comes running toward us (you may have heard the story of the prodigal son. It has been on the best seller list for a long time). At this moment I would really like to learn about any conscious step you may have taken in your adult life towards God. So far I am not having much luck.

So I do not know what to do. I do not know whether giving you a Christian burial will be for God's glory, or compromise the integrity of the Church. We all know that a funeral has absolutely nothing to do with whether we go to heaven or not. Many saints did not receive a Christian burial, but are in heaven. Other people—famous, wealthy, and powerful people—who might be buried with great pomp and ceremony but have grave, unrepented sins are not helped by their funerals, because repenting is one of the few things only we can do for ourselves. In any other sphere of life a different set of expectations is in place—if I am not in the army, for example, and ask for a military funeral the officer at the local base will not only deny my request, he will think I am crazy. But the Church, the Church is, well, supposed to be different!

"But Father, the funeral is for the living." If I hear this nonsense one more time I think I am going to be sick. Baptism is for the living. Confession is for the living. Communion is for the living. I have never heard of a funeral being served for someone who was alive. Orthodox Christians believe that prayers for the dead can be beneficial. We do not believe in closed casket funerals, or worse yet, funerals without a corpse. Yes, a funeral, piously served and chanted, with a proper sermon, can bring great comfort, spiritual edification and sometimes even enlightenment to the family and mourners present. But it is my experience that people write their own eulogy. In cases like yours lying will not do, and telling the truth might not be terribly comfortable.

So forgive me. If I was wiser, and more compassionate, and holier, I would know what to do, what to say. But I do not. Am I going to serve the funeral? I do not know yet. The only thing I know for sure is that at this moment I hope and pray with all my heart that your current dilemma is less traumatic than mine. But somehow I doubt it. ■

The Ordination

No sacrament demonstrates the health and vitality of the Church, no holy mystery brings joy and a sense of hope for the future as much as an ordination. A Church which is healthy and growing will regularly celebrate this solemn mystery. But by virtue of the fact that only a very small percentage of the faithful are "set apart" for sacramental service at the Table of the Lord the ordination service is one which most of the faithful rarely witness.

Orthodox Christianity recognizes two "levels" or "degrees" of ordination. The "lesser orders" consist of the offices of candle bearer/reader/chanter, and sub-deacon. The service to make a reader or sub-deacon takes place in the middle of the temple, before the Liturgy, at the bishop's *cathedra*. The major orders consist of the office of deacon, priest, and bishop, and ordinations to these offices are served in the altar itself during the Liturgy. The elevation of a layperson to the lesser orders is called in Greek *"Cheirothesia,"* or the "placing on" of hands. The ordination to the higher orders is called *"Cheirotonia"*—the "laying on" of hands.

What is necessary for an ordination to take place? First, and most importantly, we need God's Holy Spirit, mediated through the person of the bishop. The bishop is called *"archierei—hierarch"* or "first-priest," because only the bishop can perform all the holy mysteries. A priest, with the blessing of his bishop, can serve any of the Holy Mysteries except for ordination.

Secondly we also need a worthy candidate. This does not necessarily mean "someone with a vocation." We often hear men talk about "having a calling" or "feeling a vocation" to the priesthood. This does often take place, but the fundamental point to remember is that whether the man has a calling or not he must be worthy. We have many examples from Church history of saints who were called quite against their will to the holy priesthood, as well as men who might have "had a calling" and were ordained, but later showed themselves to be wolves in sheep's clothing rather than good pastors of God's rational flock.

Lastly, we must have a need. People are not ordained simply because they feel a vocation, have a theological education, and want to wear a cassock. The Church must have need for a deacon, priest, or bishop. Men are ordained for service in a specific community. This fact is reflected in the ordination service itself—during the ordination prayer not only the name of the candidate is mentioned, but also the name of the community which he is ordained to serve.

The ordination service, like all the other services of our Church, is notable for its deep meaning and symbolic beauty. We read in the book of Acts the apostles saying to the gathered Church *". . . seek out from among you seven men of good reputation, full of the Holy Spirit and wisdom, whom we may appoint over this business; but we will give ourselves continually to prayer and to the ministry of the word. And the saying pleased the whole multitude. And they chose Stephen, a man full of faith and the Holy Spirit, and Philip, Prochorus, Nicanor, Timon, Parmenas, and Nicolas, a proselyte from Antioch, whom they set before the apostles, and when they had prayed, they laid hands on them"* (Acts 6: 3-6).

Everything recorded about the election and ordination of the first Deacons in this passage is practiced to this very day within the Orthodox Church. There is an election, followed by prayer, and the laying on of hands.

Under normal circumstances candidates for Holy Orders are elected by the bishop(s), with greater or lesser involvement by priests and laity, depending on the particular Orthodox Church involved. Before ordination candidates are expected to make a life confession to the ordaining hierarch, who has the right to refuse ordination to the candidate without having to give a reason.

Liturgically the ordination begins with the candidate being led to the Royal Doors, and then being led around the Holy Table three times, each time reverencing the bishop and finally venerating the Holy Table itself. While the procession takes place the hymns "O Holy Martyrs , . . . " "Glory to Thee" and "Dance, Isaiah , . . . " are sung.

Following the procession the candidate kneels before the Holy Table, the bishop lays his hand and omophorion upon the head of the candidate and reads the appropriate prayers of ordination. During this time the clergy and faithful sing "Lord, have mercy" underlining the fact that it is not only the grace of the episcopate but the prayers of all the faithful which are necessary for ordination.

Finally the candidate is clothed in the vestments of his new "order," and upon receiving the particular vestments the clergy and faithful all sing "Axios!," Greek for "He is worthy!" As the ordination is begun by electing the candidate, it is finished with the whole church, clergy and laity, giving their assent to the ordination.

What is a priest ordained for? Technically speaking, a priest is a person who performs a sacrifice. In the Orthodox Church the ordained priesthood, those set apart for a specific, purely priestly function, are charged by the whole community with offering the sacrifice—the bloodless sacrifice of bread and wine. To put it simply, men are ordained so they might serve the Liturgy, offering the Eucharist ". . . *on behalf of all and for all.*"

In addition to the purely sacerdotal function of the priest, which is liturgically manifested by the laying on of hands during the ordination, there is another aspect, which is liturgically manifested by the triple procession of the candidate around the altar.

We cannot help but be struck by the fact that the exact same liturgical action with the same hymns being sung is performed during the ordination as during the wedding. As the man and the wife are married one to another, the ordination service itself explains to us that the candidate is "married" to the community he is to serve. The bishop, priest, or deacon, like a good husband or wife, is to be faithful, he must be prepared to sacrifice not only bread and wine but to sacrifice his very self for the good of his flock and the good of the Church. The issue of the bishop or priest being "married" to his flock, being in some sense "of one flesh" with them, is emphasized by Metropolitan John Zizioulas in his book Being as Communion, He writes:

"Just as the Church becomes through the ministry a relational entity both in itself and in its relation to the world, so also the ordained man becomes, through his ordination, a relational

entity. In this context, looking at the ordained person as an individual defeats the very end of ordination. For ordination . . . aims precisely at making man not an individual but a person, i.e. an ek-static being, that can be looked upon not from the angle of his "limits" but of his overcoming his "selfhood" and becoming a related being. . . . In the light of the koinonia (communion) of the Holy Spirit, ordination relates the ordained man so profoundly and so existentially to the community that in his new state after ordination he cannot be any longer, as a minister, conceived in himself. . . . Only in terms of love can one understand the mystery of charismatic life and therefore of ministry."

Those who have been fortunate enough to witness an ordination will no doubt recognize the unique blessing such an event is for the person involved, for the community, and for the whole Church. But it is also important for us to remember that just as grace can be given, it can be lost. No one "possesses" grace, the way we possess money or other material goods, able to distribute them to whomever we please.

Members of the clergy must constantly cultivate this grace that they have been given by personal prayer, study of scripture, fasting, almsgiving, humility, morality, honesty—simply put, by being *". . . an example to the believers in word, in conduct, in love, in spirit, in faith, in purity"* (1 Tim. 4:12). The grace of the priesthood is something which must be cherished and cultivated by the laity as well as the clergy. The prayers of the faithful are no less necessary for the continuing presence, guidance and action of the Holy Spirit in the life of an individual bishop, priest, or deacon than they are for the ordination ceremony itself.

Let us always remember our bishops, priests, and deacons in our prayers, and entreat God that he might continue to raise up worthy candidates to serve Him, His Church, and His children. ■

The Bread of Immortality, or a Piece of Toast?

The central act through which baptized Christians receive Divine Grace and confess their belief in Jesus Christ and His Church is the reception of Holy Communion. Faithful Orthodox Christians are especially encouraged to partake of the Most Holy Mysteries during Great Lent. For many of the faithful, however, Lent is the only time they receive Communion. If the reception of Holy Communion is so important and beneficial why do many Orthodox partake of the Eucharist only once or twice a year?

Some believe that frequent participation in the Eucharist somehow "cheapens" it. Some believe they are not worthy to commune often. Others have a problem with the idea of sacramental confession. Still others abstain simply out of habit—they like their toast and coffee in the morning, but the Eucharistic fast would preclude this.

The prayers and petitions of the Divine Liturgy clearly demonstrate an expectation that most if not all of present at Liturgy will receive communion. *"With fear of God, Faith and Love draw near!"* is a command. *"Having received the Divine, Holy, Most-pure, Immortal, Heavenly, Life-giving Mysteries, let **us** worthily give thanks , . . ."* does not make sense if only the priest has communed. In the early Church it was taken for granted that every member of the congregation, unless they had a good reason for not doing so (e.g., were under penance for a grave sin), would partake of Holy Communion at every Liturgy.

By the end of the 1st millennium we notice that while the clergy commune every time they serve the Liturgy (indeed, it is forbidden for them not to) the faithful partake of Holy Communion more and more infrequently.

In tsarist Russia, especially after Peter the Great, the Roman Catholic practice (instituted at the 4th Lateran Council in 1215) of requiring every member of the faithful to approach once a year, during Great Lent, for confession and communion, became generally accepted. Over time in many places it became the norm for the faithful to approach for confession and communion <u>only</u> once a year. In certain localities this practice has been promoted by Orthodox clergy till recent times.

During the 18th and 19th centuries both Eastern and Western Christians began to reconsider the practice of infrequent communion. The "Kollyvades" fathers in Greece, for example, began recommending frequent communion in the late 18th century, an example followed in the 19th century by Catholics and Anglicans.

The exhortation for the faithful to receive Holy Communion more frequently was based on both theology and experience. By not approaching the chalice I deprive myself of Eucharistic grace. Infrequent communion can contribute to a loss or diminution of a "sacramental mentality," (i.e., not receiving Communion can cause me to question the necessity or benefit of participating in other Mysteries of the Church.) Infrequent communion can also lead to the cultivation of a Protestant spirituality, for if I do not commune my participation in the Liturgy consists solely of worship, prayer, and intellectual stimulation—precisely what the Protestant congregation down the block offers.

For those who might think they are unworthy to receive communion often, the only thing that can be said is: "Good!" We all are. But by virtue of our Baptism and our struggle to live good, Christian lives God makes us worthy of the "heavenly bread and the cup of life," through which we receive the grace and strength necessary to live good, Christian lives.

Those who feel that receiving Holy Communion often can somehow "cheapen" the experience also have a point. In the words of Metropolitan Kallistos (Ware): ". . .*every time we receive Holy Communion it must be an event.*" This applies to clergy as well as laity. But if the sinful man presiding at the altar can experience such an event every Sunday, perhaps the faithful child, adolescent, adult, or senior citizen in the pew can as well; if not weekly, then at least monthly.

Though there is no Church canon requiring Confession before Communion, in the course of time, along with appropriate prayers and fasting, Confession has become a normal part of the preparation for receiving Holy Communion. In some parishes or traditions it is required of adults before every single reception of Communion, while in others it is less frequent, with the faithful confessing monthly or quarterly while receiving the Eucharist at most Liturgies in the interim. A person who doesn't believe in sacramental confession should stay away from the Chalice. But it is a truism that "confession is good for the soul." Every Christian (clergy first and foremost) must have a confessor/spiritual father whom they trust and to whom they can confess anything. Before approaching for confession we must reflect upon all the sins we have committed, repent of them, and then confess them vocally before the priest without excuses or rationalizations. As the patristic teaching says, "what is unrevealed remains unhealed." If we are serious about any type of spiritual growth we should be confessing and communing at least once a month.

Mostly, though, it seems that the majority of Orthodox who only commune on rare occasions do so simply out of habit. From the standpoint of the apostolic Church, sacramental theology and the teaching of the saints we would have to say it is probably not a good habit. But not-so-good habits can be broken.

So what will it be on Sunday morning—a piece of toast, or the Bread of Immortality? ■

THE CHURCH YEAR

The Rhythm of Life

Whether on the job, at school, or at recreational activities such as music, dancing or sports, one thing which is of primary importance to our employers, teachers, co-workers and team members is attendance. Attendance is one of the most basic yardsticks of everything we do, because if we are not present at work, school or practice it is virtually impossible for us to learn, to work or to play together—in a word, it is impossible to contribute. When we speak of our commitment to Christ attendance plays no less important a role—first and foremost attendance at holy services, as well as attendance at parish meetings, social events, etc.

It would not be an exaggeration to say that most services in our Churches are under attended. It is interesting to wonder how lively and active our parishes would be if parishioners treated church attendance with the same seriousness they treat attendance at their job, school, sports team or folk-dance club. We sometimes hear or read calls for "spiritual renewal," which often propose an easy fix. "Let's shorten the Liturgy," "maybe we should have hot dogs for the kids after Liturgy," and "Lets forget about all this fasting stuff" are just three suggestions which I personally have heard proposed. Our Lord described the Christian life as a narrow path, a journey requiring discipline, sacrifice and courage. There is no easy or painless way to achieve spiritual renewal or growth in our parish or personal life—but attending the services is probably the most important step if we are truly interested in seeing this growth.

The first Christian feast day was and still is Sunday. Before there were any other feast days the Christians celebrated Sunday as the commemoration of the Resurrection. To this day Sunday morning is the day when the community gathers and we celebrate the "breaking of the bread."

Some sects and denominations have in the recent past fallen away from this apostolic practice. The Seventh-day Adventists, for example, worship on Saturday, saying (correctly) that this is the Biblical Sabbath. They forget, however, that we are Christians, not Jews, and we celebrate the new Passover—the Resurrection—and neither the Passover nor the Sabbath of the Jews. This particular controversy was decided by the Church during the first centuries of her existence, and could only remain a matter of contention for those unacquainted with the authentic, historic Christian tradition.

Since the second Vatican council the Catholics have instituted Saturday evening masses—so that members who have "more important" things to do on Sunday morning can fulfill their "Sunday obligation" and not miss these commitments. Again, this is an innovation, not a part of the authentic Christian tradition.

Many protestant sects are philosophically bereft of any reason for going to Church on Sunday morning at all. If it is true, as they contend, that all you have to do to be saved is to accept Jesus as your personal Savior this very nicely does away with both the "Sunday obligation" and any other type of obligation as well!

While we are forbidden to judge others we can say without hesitation that in contrast to the Western denominations Orthodox Christianity possesses the fullness of the apostolic Christian teaching and practice. The participation of the faithful in the Liturgy is not an onerous obligation but a divinely granted privilege, and is in fact constitutive of the Church. This is what the apostles taught by word and deed, and this is what we believe. If we wish to have a truly healthy Church the first step that each and every member of the Church must take is forming in themselves an attitude towards Church attendance which is at least as serious as their attitude towards attendance at their job, school, service organization meeting or dance class.

Besides the Sunday Liturgy the Orthodox Church celebrates many other feast days as well. Some of them, Pascha and Pentecost for example, always fall on Sundays. Others, the so-called "immovable" feasts, always fall on the same date, the best known of these being Christmas—the feast of the Nativity of Our Lord. The vast majority of non-Orthodox denominations do not celebrate or even admit the existence of these traditional and historic feast days. Even those who retain the traditional calendar of feasts and fasts, such as the Roman Catholic Church, have in most cases given these feasts and fasts a purely symbolic meaning. The Roman Catholic Church in Canada, for example, has "transferred" almost all feast days to the nearest Sunday. Several years ago, while conversing about feast days with a devout Catholic, I was amused to hear him say "we will be celebrating Ascension Thursday next Sunday!"

As is obvious from the word itself, the original meaning of holiday is "Holy day"—a Church feast day. Besides attendance at holy services one of the traditional ways of marking a holy day is to refrain from work. If we look at the current celebration of civil holidays we see that they are generally regarded simply as a day off of work—a Christian hand-me-down to our secular society. Consequently, due to the fact that the festal calendar of the Church has been to a large degree suppressed by the western denominations, we live in a society which has almost totally divested itself of any authentic Christian consciousness regarding holidays.

The Orthodox Church maintains the original, authentic understanding of "Holidays," some of which—the commemoration of the death of martyrs or the feast of the Resurrection for example—date from the first century, and others—such as the feast of the Protection of the Most Holy Theotokos—which are of later origin. The development of the Church Calendar, just like the development of Holy Scripture, is witnessed to in the life, history and legislation of the Orthodox Church—we know what we celebrate, when we celebrate, and why we celebrate. And most importantly, the Orthodox Church has never seen fit to ignore or suppress feast days, but sees the celebration of a feast in the same light She sees the blessing of water or oil or the faithful—as the sanctification of that which God has created for us, in this case the sanctification of time.

Understanding this, the celebration of feast days by participation in the Divine Liturgy is for the Orthodox a very important sign of our faith, especially in our North American social context. Even more so than attendance at Sunday Liturgy, attendance at Feast-day Liturgies is a sign of real commitment not just to some kind of indistinct "Christianity," but to true, historical Orthodox

Christian Faith. Just as we give of our money and talents for the good of God's Church, we give of our time and our gratitude and our worship. We are called upon to be a worshiping people—and this we do first and foremost in Church on Sundays and Holy days—i.e., on the days God has set aside for us to do so.

At this point someone might say "yes, father, this is all well and good, but in this day and age it is not practical to take a day off of work or school to attend services." I remember well a conversation I had a few years ago with a young mother who was also a school-teacher. I had suggested that it might be nice if parents occasionally booked the morning off from work to attend feast-day services with their children. She dismissed this as impractical. I asked her if she took off time for vacations, for doctor's appointments, or just "mental health days." The answer to every question was "yes." I then repeated the thought, that it would be nice for parents to take off one morning, even if only once a year, to attend services on a weekday with their children. She looked at me as if I were from Mars! She could understand taking a month of paid vacation for herself or her family, but could not understand taking even 4 (paid) hours, once a year, to worship God with her children on a weekday morning.

Others might say "In the old country people did not have anything better to do than attend Church services." I find the argument that our ancestors had "nothing better to do" than go to Church extremely amusing—and whether it is the "old country" or America, the reason is the same. Try spending a year living and working on a farm with no electricity, running water, gasoline engines or social safety net, being dependent upon what you can harvest from the earth for your very life. Try carrying all your water 3 or 6 or 9 blocks from a well, or baking all your bread every day in a wood-fired oven from grain you have sown, harvested, threshed, and probably even ground. The fact of the matter is that our ancestors had much less "personal" time than we have at our disposal, and certainly no paid vacations. Perhaps they simply had more faith in God?

Why should I attend services on feast days? Any priest or pious layman can give you many theological and practical reasons why the faithful should attend festal liturgies if at all possible. One of the reasons often overlooked is that attendance at these liturgies permits us to understand our Faith from another perspective. Attending Liturgy on Holy days permits us to enter into the rhythm of the life of the Church.

The rhythm of Church life has three components—the daily, weekly and yearly cycles. The daily cycle for an average Orthodox Christian in the world usually consists of prayers upon arising, prayers before sleep, and prayer before and after meals. This might be expanded by personally reading through one of the shorter services or praying on the prayer rope. The weekly and yearly cycles, however, require a liturgical participation to truly experience them. While we can speak of personal prayer or devotion, it is impossible to speak of a "personal" liturgical experience. If the Divine Services truly are important for our salvation then the faithful must take part in them. This participation is different for everyone. Only the monk or nun will be able to participate fully in the daily cycle of services, but the weekly and yearly cycle of worship is accessible to all the faithful who live within reasonable proximity to a Church.

Music has three basic parts: melody, harmony and rhythm. Rhythm is the basis of all music, the foundation upon which melody and harmony are built. Likewise the life of the Church—which we understand to be a foretaste of life in paradise—is built on a concrete rhythm, the rhythm of the Church calendar, of the feasts and of the fasts. Beginning with attendance at worship every Sunday, and building up to the attendance at all services throughout the year, we are given a chance to take our lives out of the rhythm of the world—the mundane—and enter into the rhythm of Paradise.

Practically speaking, this is one of the important reasons for serving Great Vespers before every feast. It is probably unrealistic to expect all the faithful to take days off to attend Liturgy the morning of every feast day (though it is a lot easier for us to do than we often care to admit), and like it or not many people are forced to work on Sunday morning. Serving Vespers gives all the faithful the opportunity to experience the rhythm of the Church year in their lives, by attending services the evening before Sunday or feast day even if they cannot attend the Liturgy.

Making time to attend the festal services as a family and as a community will strengthen our faith, our families and our parishes more than we can imagine. The Jews have lived their religious life according to a different calendar for millennia. This simple fact has exerted an immense influence on their continued existence. When our Churches are as full every Sunday as they are on Pascha, and when they are as full on Holy days as they are now on Sunday, we will see a spiritual revival in our parishes and in our Church—a revival the scale of which we probably cannot imagine.

As any builder knows, the most important part of the house is the foundation. Our Lord Himself spoke of this, saying that the one who follows His commandments is like the one who builds their house on a rock. (cf. Matt. 7:24-8:4) If the Church truly is Christ's body, as St. Paul says, (cf. Col. 1:18, Rom. 12:4, 1 Cor. 12:12, *et cetera.*) then Her commandments are the commandments of Christ. And if we wish to build our lives on a firm foundation, what foundation can be more solid than the mystical life of the Church? By making the rhythm of the Church the rhythm of our own personal life we will certainly see marked spiritual growth in our lives and communities, and upon this foundation we will be able to more deeply experience the melody of prayer and the harmony of true Christian life. ∎

"If Christ is not Risen. . . ."

"Orthodoxy sees humanity's problem as its bondage to sin, death and the devil. . . . What is assured in Christ's incarnation, pursued in his life and reached for in his death—namely, eternal life, communion with God and victory over our enemies—is only achieved fully and completely when Christ rises from the grave. . . . in Eastern Orthodoxy. . . . Easter is celebrated as the great day in which salvation is assured and achieved. The Easter vigil service in an Orthodox Church is an elaborate, overwhelmingly joyful celebration. Anyone who attends such a service will have no doubt about the primary importance ascribed by the Orthodox to the resurrection of Christ for our salvation" (Dr. James Payton, Light from the Christian East, p. 129).

Dr. Payton in his wonderful book reminds us of something we Orthodox often take for granted—the "Resurrection-centredness" of our faith. Death is the central and inexorable fact of our biological existence. We have all probably experienced the death of a loved one, and unless we live till the second coming of Christ we will certainly die ourselves. The way we conduct our life depends entirely upon our convictions regarding death.

For many people Easter is simply an opportunity to spend time with family and friends. For others it is a chance to self-identify with a particular culture or tradition. For still others it is just a myth.

For Christians, Pascha—Christ's Resurrection and victory over death—is the very foundation of our faith. St. Paul says *". . . . if Christ is not risen, then our preaching is empty and your faith is also empty. Yes, and we are found false witnesses of God, because we have testified of God that He raised up Christ, whom He did not raise up – if in fact the dead do not rise. For if the dead do not rise, then Christ is not risen. And if Christ is not risen, your faith is futile; you are still in your sins! Then also those who have fallen asleep in Christ have perished. If in this life only we have hope in Christ, we are of all men the most pitiable"* (1 Cor. 15:14–19).

As St. Paul emphasizes, if Christ is not risen our loved ones have perished. They will not rise. They, and eventually we, simply cease to exist, leaving no trace in a universe that itself will perish. If Christ is not risen our faith is nonsense. As far as "religion" understood as a human phenomenon is concerned Christianity has nothing to offer but the Resurrection. If Christ is not risen our sacraments are a sham—how can bread and wine become the body and blood of a resurrected Christ who has not been raised bodily? If Christ is not risen our sins are not forgiven; there is no justice for perpetrators of evil or their victims; if Christ is not risen we have no hope.

As C.S. Lewis notes in Miracles, *"In the earliest days of Christianity an 'apostle' was first and foremost a man who claimed to be an eyewitness of the Resurrection."* (cf. Acts 1:22; 1 Cor. 9:1)

Countless martyrs to this very day have sacrificed their lives not for a religion, but for a Person. They, as the apostles before them, claim to have in some mysterious way seen the risen Christ, experienced the reality of the Resurrection, and became convinced that He lives, reigns, and acts. For them the reality of Christ was more real than the greatest pleasures or the worst tortures this world can offer.

"Let us purify our senses, and in the unapproachable light of the resurrection we shall see Christ shining forth, and we shall clearly hear Him saying, 'Rejoice!' as we sing a song of victory" (Paschal Canon, 1st canticle).

The victory which Orthodox Christians celebrate so joyfully in the Paschal services is victory over sin and death. We are able to see Christ, experience this victory, and rejoice to the degree that our senses are purified—i.e., to the extent that we fulfill the commandments of God and the teaching of Christ.

If Christ truly is risen, if our Paschal joy is grounded in reality and truth, then the dead still somehow live, and we will be raised bodily with them.

If Christ truly is risen "forgiveness has dawned forth from the tomb."

If Christ truly is risen our most trivial and seemingly insignificant words, deeds and thoughts are infinitely important, as they and their consequences will remain with us eternally.

If Christ truly is risen unrepentant sinners and evildoers will suffer the eternal consequences of Divine Justice.

If Christ truly is risen those who love God and fulfill His commandments will enjoy perpetual communion with Him, and our prayers, worship, sacraments, deeds of mercy—everything we do out of love for Christ and neighbor—will shine forever before the throne of God.

May we joyfully celebrate Christ's victory over sin and death not only on Pascha, but every Sunday. May the light of the Resurrection permeate every facet of our life, giving us the strength and hope necessary to respond to the trials, difficulties, illness and death which are an inescapable part of life in this world.

"O Great and most holy Pascha, Christ! O Wisdom and Word of God and Power! Grant that we may partake of You fully in the never-ending day of Your Kingdom!" (Paschal Canon, 9th canticle). ∎

A Canonical Calendrical Conundrum

The Orthodox usually celebrate the feast of the Resurrection of our Lord—Pascha—either one, four, or five weeks after the date commonly observed by Catholics and Protestants. One of the questions often asked of an Orthodox priest is "why do the Orthodox celebrate Easter at a different time from everyone else?"

The Julian ("old" or "church") calendar is thirteen days out of sync with the Gregorian (new or civil) calendar. All Christians celebrate Christmas on December 25th, for example, but December 25th on the old calendar falls thirteen days later— i.e., January 7th according to the new calendar. All "immovable" feast days, (i.e., those which are celebrated on a fixed date every year like the Nativity, Theophany, Annunciation, St. Nicholas) are celebrated 13 days later by those Orthodox who follow the old calendar.

Apart from the immovable feast days all Christians follow a calendar of "moveable" feasts, which are based on the date of Easter. All the Sundays of the year, as well as the periods of the Triodion (the 10 weeks preceding Pascha) and the Pentecostarion (the services from Easter till the Sunday of All Saints) fall into this category of "moveable" feasts.

One of the issues which was discussed and decided upon at the First Ecumenical Council in Nicaea in 325 A.D. was the procedure for finding the date of Easter. Until that time two practices were being followed. The "Quartodeciman" practice was to celebrate Pascha according to the Jewish calendar. Based on the Gospel accounts of Christ's passion we know the dates of Jesus' death and Resurrection. The 14th day of the Jewish month of Nisan was the date upon which this group celebrated Pascha (the word "quartodeciman" comes from the Latin word for fourteen). Consequently, this group celebrated Pascha on different days of the week, not necessarily on a Sunday, dependent upon the Jewish calendar date. The other practice was to always celebrate the Resurrection on a Sunday, because we know that Jesus was raised on "the first day of the week."

At the First Ecumenical Council the decision was made to celebrate Pascha a) on the first Sunday, b) after the first full moon, c) after the spring equinox, d) after the Passover (Pascha) of the Jews. This was not an arbitrary choice—every condition has a historical, practical and theological foundation. The reason for not celebrating before or with the Jews, for example, has to do with the fact that the Jewish Passover is the old Pascha, and Christ's Passover from death to life is the New Pascha, and the old always precedes the new.

This paschal unity was kept by the entire Church and after the Roman schism by the Roman Catholics and Protestants as well until 1582. In that year Pope Gregory changed the calendar. The Julian calendar loses approximately three days every four hundred years in relation to the solar year. By 1582 A.D. the Julian calendar had fallen 10 days out of sync with the calendar which had been used at the first ecumenical council. The date of the spring equinox in 325 A.D. was March 21st, and by 1582 it was falling on March 11th, even though it "officially" still fell on the 21st as far as the calendar date was concerned. One of the goals of the calendar change was, in fact, to "stabilize the equinox" on March 21st.

The reconciliation of the calendar to astronomical reality was only one part of the reform. The other part, the part unacceptable to the Orthodox, was the change of the Paschalion, the formula used to calculate the date of Easter. In fixing the date for Easter, the astronomers engaged by Pope Gregory ignored the fourth condition, namely, that the Christian Pascha cannot be celebrated either with or before the Jewish Pascha. This is why the Latin Easter often precedes the Jewish Passover.

The Gregorian calendrical reform was not accepted by any Orthodox Churches, and was explicitly condemned by councils in 1583, 1587 and 1593. All Orthodox Churches followed the Julian calendar until 1923, when a council was held in Constantinople which accepted the use of the "Reformed Julian Calendar,"(i.e., the use of the new calendar for all immoveable feasts —celebrating Christmas on December 25th rather than January 7th), but following the old calendar for the moveable feasts, those dependent upon the date of Pascha.

Only the Churches of Constantinople, Greece, Romania and Serbia were represented at this council, and only the Churches of Constantinople, Greece, and Romania accepted the use of this "Reformed Julian Calendar." In the course of time other Churches accepted this change, so that at the present time, in addition to those mentioned above, the Churches of Bulgaria, Finland, Alexandria, Antioch, and portions of the Church of Poland and the OCA (former Russian Metropolia in North America) use the new calendar.

So what is our "canonical calendrical conundrum?" In certain years (2002, for example) we see that Roman Catholics and Old-Calendar Orthodox celebrate Pascha canonically—that is, in accordance with the canons of their respective churches. In 2002 Roman Catholics, for whom the spring equinox falls on March 21st, celebrated Easter on March 31st, the first Sunday after the first full moon after the 21st. The Old-Calendar Orthodox, for whom the spring equinox "officially" fell on April 3rd (which is March 21st according to the Old Calendar) celebrated Pascha on the 5th of May (N.S.), the 1st Sunday after the first full moon after April 3rd. Those Orthodox who use the "Revised Julian Calendar," however, celebrated Pascha on the Sunday after the 2nd full moon after the equinox—something clearly "uncanonical!"

At this juncture several points need to be made. First of all, the situation in which those who follow the old calendar find themselves is clearly artificial. The equinox is not a date on a calendar but a fact in the sky. Secondly, the choice of those Orthodox who follow the new calendar to adhere to the old calendar Paschalion is clearly a choice made in order to maintain the Paschal unity of the whole Church, and as such we should be thankful for this. But thirdly, and most importantly, we must all recognize that the situation is abnormal, and try to again regain full calendrical unity.

The only way to do so is the Orthodox way—to call a council. The bishops of all the local Churches must gather together and decide which course is to be followed. Are all to return to the use of the old calendar? Will everyone agree to follow the new calendar? If so, will the Paschalion be revised? In such a case the date for Easter would usually, but not always, coincide with the Latin celebration.

The current dichotomy of usage causes pastoral problems for the Church as well. Many families belonging to parishes following the old calendar are often forced to celebrate great holidays like the Nativity or Theophany in the absence of children who are away at school. Besides the obvious astronomical inconsistency of the Julian calendar, the common understanding that those on the old calendar "celebrate Christmas twice," and the various ways this phenomenon manifests itself in parish and family life are themselves a very strong argument for calendrical reform. Under normal circumstances it is difficult to follow the Nativity fast, but for those following the Julian Calendar they not only have the challenge of dealing with Christmas parties before Christmas, they cannot truly celebrate with close friends or relatives who will invite them to celebrate Christmas or New Year on the new calendar. While it is true that the Old Calendar gives some "insulation" from our non-Orthodox and non-Christian society, it is also true that it gives our society, composed of children of God who need to hear His Word and be saved, insulation from the True Christian Faith.

Should the calendar be revised? This is a decision that only the Church, gathered in council under the guidance of the Holy Spirit, can answer. Should we have a Church calendar which is commonly utilized by all Orthodox Churches? The Fathers of the First Ecumenical Council certainly thought so, and with good reason. Until such time as this desirable and necessary goal is reached we should do our best to understand why we celebrate when we do, and pray that God will grant our Patriarchs, Bishops, clergy and lay leaders the wisdom and humility to act in a unified manner for the good of the Church and the salvation of His people. ∎

The Biggest "C" in Christmas

Christmas—the feast of the Nativity of Our Lord—tends to bring out the many and varied understandings that people have regarding the Christian faith. When it comes to both Christmas and Christianity there are lots of "dead ends"—paths which do not go anywhere, attached to the main road, which often fulfil an important function but which, if treated as ends in themselves, will not get us where we want to go.

I would like to suggest six "C's" whose presence is ubiquitous during the Christmas season which fall into this category, as well as a seventh which gives meaning to them all.

Church. We all know that people generally attend Church services more at Christmastime. The "C & E" (Christmas and Easter) crowd, though large, is fleeting. Many people seem to expect that the Church will be there for them, year in and year out, without thinking too much about the fact that someone has to pay the bills, look after the maintenance, fill out reports.

Others are involved in the Church on a day-to-day basis, engaged in administration, active in organizational life, working with youth, helping out wherever and however they can. For some people these activities become an end in themselves.

Whether our Church membership is completely nominal or totally active we must never forget that Christmas is not simply about "Church."

Cuisine. All of our Orthodox countries of origin have very beautiful traditions surrounding the celebration of the Nativity of our Lord. Most of these involve food. The Ukrainians, for example, have the beautiful and meaningful "Holy Supper" on Christmas Eve. This Holy Supper for some people, though, is nothing more than an opportunity to eat "Ukrainian Soul Food." We even see that family members attend the Holy Supper but do not attend worship services!

Whether our family origins are in Ukraine, Greece, or the U.S. of A. we must not forget that Jesus was not born simply so that we might eat perogies, or baklava, or roast turkey with all the trimmings.

Culture. Who among us has not enjoyed the music of Christmas carolers? Who has not been filled with joy during the performance of a Christmas play? Language, music, folk customs and even literary works (e.g. the public readings of "The Night Before Christmas" in our civil society, or the often elaborate and beautiful performances of our ethnic carolers) are a mainstay of our Nativity celebrations. A tree cut off from its roots, though, is bound to die. What is the root of our "Christmas Culture"? What truth does it express?

Clan. Songs like "I'll be home for Christmas" or "Christmas is for Children" became popular for good reason—it is a time of year when people gather together as family, no matter what their faith or lack thereof. This custom, which is good in and of itself, can also be cut off from its roots. I heard not long ago about a family who had "Sviat Vechir" (the Ukrainian Christmas Eve celebration) in August! As with many families, the children were scattered all over the globe due to work, career, etc. The only time everyone could get together was in August. They decided, therefore, that they would have their Christmas Eve dinner at this time.

No one would disagree that it is a good idea for families to spend time together as often as possible. But the Nativity is a feast day of the Church. Turning the celebration of the Nativity of Christ primarily into a family centered, rather than a Church centered celebration is problematic for obvious reasons.

Country. Here in Canada we are proud of our Ukrainian heritage. One of the biggest opportunities we get to "self-identify" as Ukrainians is the celebration of our holidays according to the Julian Calendar. For over a century our friends and neighbors here have heard about "Ukrainian Christmas," and the same is true for the Russians, the Serbians, and all those who celebrate on the old calendar. But Jesus was not born so that we might have an opportunity to cultivate pride in our cultural heritage, our country of origin, or a calendar which is not quite accurate.

Community. It is sad that in our contemporary Western society the importance of community is more and more being eroded. Due to employment, economic factors, the suburban lifestyle, geographic dispersion, the cult of privacy, the Internet, etc. we see more and more people living a solitary and secluded life. The Church, thank God, exists (among other things) to be community. There is no salvation in isolation. But reducing our religious life only to community, where we socialize with friends, do good works together, help and support one another, and so forth, turns it into just another club, nothing more than a free association of like-minded individuals.

Church, Cuisine, Culture, Clan, Country, and Community are all very important. But from the standpoint of our faith there is one more "C," more important than any other, which gives meaning to all of them. As you may have guessed, it is **Christ**.

Without Christ there is no Church. He is, as the saying goes, the "reason for the season"—but that is not all. He is the reason for everything, for the altruism we show towards one another, for the beautiful culture we are heirs of, for the love of God and neighbor we share at this Christmas season.

As we celebrate His birth, let us never forget that without Him we can do nothing. (cf. John 15:5) That the joy we feel is only meaningful and lasting insofar as it is the joy He gives us. (cf. John 16:24) And that only with Christ will our Christmas Eve suppers, parish gatherings, carols, families, churches and celebrations be blessed and holy, full of eternal meaning and heavenly joy. ■

Summer Vacation

As we approach the end of the school year and the beginning of the "vacation season" we approach one of the most difficult and dangerous periods of our church year. In parishes all over the continent thousands and thousands of parishioners will be "taking vacations" from the divine services. Some will do so because they are out of town, visiting relatives, sightseeing; some will do so because they are away at camp or summer courses; but many will not be in church simply because it is summertime. Why is this a great problem, and what can we do to address it?

As faithful Orthodox Christians we are called upon to live lives of responsibility and commitment. We also understand that our primary responsibility and commitment is to God and the Church. This Christian responsibility and commitment often exists in tension with our secular culture. Perhaps one of the greatest examples of this tension is the attitude which has grown up around church attendance in the summer months. Because children have a vacation from school and parents from work, because many go to the cottage or on vacation, we apply this same attitude to our religious obligations and "take a vacation" from Church. As all of us know, there is nothing in our Holy Scripture or Holy Tradition to support such a practice. It is a practice unique to our modern, western culture. It exists basically because of laziness and a poor understanding of our faith. This is a very dangerous habit to have, both for our salvation and for the growth and "good estate" of our Church.

Is it bad to go on vacation for weeks or months during the summer? Obviously not. But how does an Orthodox Christian go on vacation? In most parts of North America an Orthodox Church of some jurisdiction exists within a reasonable driving distance. Finding a church is no more difficult than looking in the yellow pages, or doing a search on the Internet. If I cannot attend at my own parish it is important to attend at the nearest parish—whether of "my own" or of another jurisdiction. This is in fact a very good habit to have, for in visiting other parishes we always notice differences—things which might be good to introduce or try in my home parish, things which we do at home which perhaps we should not, and things which really make me appreciate my home parish. In any case, if I can spend the time and money to travel hundreds or thousands of miles on vacation, traveling 30 or 60 minutes on a Sunday morning to give glory to the God who gave me the means to go on vacation should not be a big deal.

Many of our young people attend Church camps. These camping programs are one of the greatest things we can offer our young people. Thank God that our Orthodox camps are by and large well looked after by our clergy, and the youth are able to participate in the divine services, not only on Sundays, but during the week as well. When our children attend camps where religious services are not offered (computer camps, sports camps, music camps) parents should make every effort to see to it that their children have some type of religious support—driving to the camp and taking their children to church on Sunday morning, for example. And in any circumstances where church attendance is simply not possible, we should then do what our forebears and pioneers here in Canada and America did—gather together as well as we can on Sunday morning and pray together from our prayer books.

In general we see that our parishes are emptier during the summer than the numbers of vacationers and campers indicate they should be. As was mentioned above, this is due to a poor understanding of what our Divine services are, and it is a very dangerous habit to have. The idea of "taking a vacation from Church" puts our attendance at Divine services in the same category as work, school, and other "unpleasant" realities, which we "need to get away from" in order to "relax, and enjoy life."

We must never forget that our divine services—the Sunday Divine Liturgy first and foremost—are our God-given opportunity to learn from, praise, and commune with God. The idea of "taking a vacation" from such an opportunity, whether one is a clergyman or layman, is simply nonexistent in our Orthodox tradition, and nonsensical from the standpoint of our Faith. When anyone consciously decides that they need not attend - or worse yet, that they will receive a real benefit by not attending Divine Services ("I will not be in Church in July and August, but I will come back refreshed and renewed in September"), they weaken the Church as well as their own spiritual constitution. The only one who benefits by such behavior is the devil.

Another danger is one which directly impacts the future of our Church. During the summer months our young people who are on vacation from school have the opportunity to more fully enter into the life of the Church, they have the opportunity to take part not only in the Sunday services, but in some of the most beautiful feast days of the Church year as well. If they stay away or are kept away from the services they cannot learn about their faith where they should—in Church. During the summer months we celebrate Pentecost, Ss. Peter and Paul, the Transfiguration and the Dormition, and often celebrate patronal parish feast days as well; since school is out, there is no excuse for those students who are not away at camp to not be in Church. These great feast days, which brought great spiritual consolation and strength to our forebears, will not bring us God's blessings if we ignore them. How many of our young people have never seen the Church bedecked in greenery for Pentecost, or the blessing of the first-fruits at the Transfiguration?

Lack of attendance at the services is always a negative factor in parish life. Those who count the money know that donations are generally down in the summer (the parish bills still need to be paid whether I am on vacation or not); those who attend liturgy every Sunday ask themselves "if they are not attending, why should I?" and clergy become demoralized and think "who am I serving this Liturgy for, the pews?"

After having celebrated Pascha, as we begin to enjoy the warmth of Spring, we should consider the fact that over the next four months a great opportunity is set before us. How will we respond? What is the example will we give to our children? ■

Why Worship?

People often talk about how the state of the world has deteriorated over recent decades. This is nothing new. St. Paul, in the first century, talks about people who are *". . . filled with all unrighteousness, sexual immorality, wickedness, covetousness, maliciousness; full of envy, murder, strife, deceit, evil-mindedness; they are whisperers, backbiters, haters of God, violent, proud, boasters, inventors of evil things, disobedient to parents, undiscerning, untrustworthy, unloving, unforgiving, unmerciful; who, knowing the righteous judgment of God, that those who practice such things are deserving of death, not only do the same but also approve of those who practice them"* (Rom. 1: 29-32).

Reading these words, we might say "he certainly knew what life was going to be like in 21st century North America!
What causes people created in the image and likeness of God to degenerate into little more than animals, if not outright monsters? St. Paul explains earlier in the chapter: *"For the wrath of God is revealed from heaven against all ungodliness and unrighteousness of men, who suppress the truth in unrighteousness, because what may be known of God is manifest in them, for God has shown it to them. For since the creation of the world His invisible attributes are clearly seen, being understood by the things that are made, even His eternal power and Godhead, so that they are without excuse. Because although they knew God they did not glorify Him as God nor were thankful . . . ."* (Rom. 1: 18: 21). *"They did not glorify Him as God nor were thankful. . . ."* The original Greek says *"edoxasan kai eucharistisan."* If St. Paul is to be believed people who do not offer God *doxa* (glory) and *eucharistia* (thanksgiving) risk becoming less than human. If what St. Paul writes is true, given the decline in Church attendance throughout North America over the past five

decades, should we be surprised at the current state of morality and interpersonal dysfunction in our society?"

If we trust Biblical teaching, the source of all troubles is the refusal to offer God glory and thanksgiving, which is what we go to Church to do in a very particular and specific way. Our choice as human beings is either to offer God glory and thanksgiving, or to be *"unloving, unforgiving, lovers of self. . . . "*

Many people feel that they do not need to go to Church to be a good person. "Can I not give God glory and thanksgiving anywhere—on the beach, on a forest trail, or in a rowboat?" It is not accidental that the Greek word for thanksgiving is "eucharistia"—"eucharist." As we know, the eucharist is not served at home, or at the beach, or in the forest, but in Church.

"This is eternal life, that they may know You, the only true God, and Jesus Christ, whom you have sent" (John 17: 3). One of the most important ways in which the people of God come to know Him is through worship and participation in the Holy Mysteries. On the other hand if we refuse to worship God we will begin to worship anything: sports teams, for example, whose temple is the stadium or arena; celebrities, whose scriptures are the magazines you see in the check-out aisle at the grocery store; money, whose sacrament is the stock exchange or the casino; sex, (no comment); or the body, whose liturgy is served at the health club. All these can be and often are objects of non-religious, but nonetheless real, worship.

In most congregations of our Church it is a sad fact that most members do not attend Church services faithfully (i.e., regularly and often). I am personally aware of people who hold leadership positions in the Church, who sit on seminary boards, are members of parish councils, but only attend Sunday Liturgy sporadically, who might partake of the Holy Supper at home on Christmas Eve but do not necessarily go to the Nativity Liturgy, who do not attend a single service during Holy Week but go to Church to have their baskets blessed or "steal the light" on Pascha.

Many excuses are given by people who do not attend Church regularly: "I do not understand what is going on," "it is boring," "I am too busy," "I have to work." Some of these excuses are valid, but most are not. There are people who do not attend Church during the school year because their children are too busy, but during the summer they do not attend because they need to "take a break." It would seem that attending Church services is not an important enough matter to be taken seriously during the school year, but is too serious to focus on during summer vacation.

So youth do not attend Church services regularly and often. And we are astonished at the amount of crime, amorality, social disintegration, and family dysfunction that we hear about on the news, read about in the paper, or experience first-hand. Amoral, criminal, and socially dysfunctional young people grow up to be amoral, criminal, and socially dysfunctional adults. Why? Among other things, because "they neither know God, nor worship Him as God."

If we truly wish to live in a better world perhaps the most important thing we can do is to attend Liturgy and other worship services with the same diligence and joy we attend sporting events, musical lessons, concerts, the theater, the casino, cultural events, work, and school. Remember—Churches are like prescriptions. They do not do you any good unless you fill them. ∎

MORAL ISSUES

Who gets the Church?

"Christianity teaches that marriage is for life. There is, of course, a difference here between different Churches: some do not admit divorce at all; some allow it reluctantly in very special cases. It is a great pity that Christians should disagree about such a question; but for an ordinary layman the thing to notice is that the Churches all agree with one another about marriage a great deal more than any of them agrees with the outside world. I mean, they all regard divorce as something like cutting up a living body, as a kind of surgical operation. Some of them think the operation so violent that it cannot be done at all; others admit it as a desperate remedy in extreme cases. They are all agreed that it is more like having both your legs cut off than it is like dissolving a business partnership or even deserting a regiment. What they all disagree with is the modern view that it is a simple readjustment of partners, to be made whenever people feel they are no longer in love with one another, or when either of them falls in love with someone else" (C.S. Lewis, <u>Mere Christianity</u>).

We all know that divorce is not a good thing. Sometimes it is necessary, but even in such cases no sane person would argue that divorce is good in and of itself. No one, given the choice, would willingly choose to go through this experience. While divorce is permitted—Jesus mentions in the Gospel, for example, that divorce is allowed in cases of sexual immorality (cf. Matt. 5:32, 19:9)—it is seen as a last resort, and accepted only grudgingly.

Within Western society the institution of marriage is under attack. Marriage has lost its value and meaning for a large part of our society. Where people still value marriage at all it is often understood in a completely personal, even selfish manner. A means of "self-fulfillment," respected in so far as and only as long as both spouses decide that it is good for them *personally*, with no commitment to spend the rest of one's natural life together *"in sickness and health, for richer or poorer"*—this is the attitude one often finds among friends and acquaintances.

Divorce has become commonplace. So, unfortunately, have its consequences: the financial burden it brings, the psychological agony, the damage it does to children, friendships, families and relationships. No less devastating are the spiritual repercussions of divorce.

We all have an idea of what "Christian Marriage" means. But is there such a thing as "Christian Divorce"? After divorce, is it possible for the couple to continue to attend the same parish? The courts will decide who gets the house, the car, the pension funds, and the children. But who gets the Church?

A couple in my parish was breaking up. It was months, if not years in the making. I heard that they had separated second hand. They never called, asked for help, sought counseling, or even indicated that there was a problem. One day it is: "How is everyone doing?" "Fine, father." And then boom! It is not a family anymore.

It is my experience that many parishioners do not feel the need to seek the Church's opinion, counsel, or help in such matters. Most parishioners, in step with secular society, feel that they, individually, are the only ones competent to arbitrate their own "personal" affairs. But the issue of divorce is an issue of great spiritual depth which affects a circle of people much greater than the couple involved. Divorce is always the result of sin, and can easily be sinful in and of itself.

It is probably fair to say that insofar as a couple is trying to live in accordance with the principles of the Gospel, they will be able to have a Christian marriage, and the more successful they are at following the commandments of Christ the less chance they will have of a marital breakdown. If for some reason a breakdown does occur, it is these same principles which will help the couple to either work through the problems or at least split up without hatred and acrimony.

It is recommended that every Orthodox Christian have a spiritual father. In the cases of families it is recommended that the entire family—husband, wife, and children—have the same spiritual father to whom they not only confess, but whose counsel they seek whenever there are problems, questions, or life decisions of great importance. A pious, Christian marriage counselor can be a valuable resource in trying to help a couple through a problem in their relationship—but regular recourse to the spiritual father coupled with regular and frequent confession and communion can help prevent difficulties from becoming problems.

But problems do occur. When divorce occurs among Orthodox Christians the first thing those involved should do is approach for confession. Generally speaking a penance (*epitimia*) may be imposed, depending upon the circumstances and the particular reasons for the divorce. This penance will usually consist of a particular rule of prayer, perhaps a time of fasting, and in the cases of grave sin, like adultery, a period of exclusion from Holy Communion. Should either partner desire in the future to remarry permission from the Bishop or Church court is necessary.

What can fellow parishioners do to help divorced or divorcing partners? The most important thing is probably to remain neutral. As the old saying goes, "no matter how thin you slice the baloney, it still has two sides!" Being Christians, we always try to take God's side. None of us is perfect, all of us are sinful, and while there are situations in which divorce might be warranted—in cases of abuse, neglect, adultery, or addiction, for example—many, perhaps most cases of divorce nowadays are a result of immaturity, financial problems, or self-centeredness. Friends, acquaintances and fellow parishioners often have the knowledge and the perspective to give beneficial advice to those having marriage difficulties, to direct them towards those who might help, to pray for them, and to support good, Christian decisions.

Nothing seems to build up hatred and acrimony as much as the dividing up of the household. The worst is when children must be split. The best gift a father can give his children is to love their mother, and I am sure the converse is true as well. Jesus speaks in the Gospel about giving good gifts to our children, (cf. Matt. 7:11) but I have yet to see children who were affected positively by a divorce. Parents who claim to be Christians have an absolute duty never to poison their children with hatred towards anyone, and friends, family, and fellow parishioners must be exceptionally compassionate towards the children of divorce.

Although most couples put on a brave face, divorce often makes people feel like failures. If the husband and wife were not simply being dishonest at their marriage ceremony, they hoped that they would be together forever—and how often do we hear these exact words at weddings? Although the social stigma of being divorced is not as pronounced as it once was, the feelings of regret, hurt, loneliness, insecurity, failure, and the financial instability which usually follows a divorce can easily lead a person to depression.

The positive role of family, friends, and fellow parishioners in supporting the divorced probably cannot be overemphasized. It is precisely in such circumstances that the need for God's help is felt most strongly. Those going through a marital breakup or recently divorced probably need the Church more than those in stable family environments. It is up to the priest and parishioners to make the parish a place of comfort for them.

Several years ago the government of Canada legally permitted marriage between homosexual partners. Many Canadians decried this innovation as a devaluation and denigration of the institution of marriage. But how can we, as Christians, say that same-sex marriage is a travesty if we ourselves devaluate marriage so greatly by accepting divorce as something "normal?"

Prevention is the best medicine. Priests must be diligent in their preparation of couples for marriage. Parents and church school teachers must see that children and youth are taught about the holiness, meaning and benefit of Christian marriage. And there is no better lesson than the example of couples who, in spite of their problems and personal idiosyncrasies, stay together through thick and thin, proving that love is not simply a word, or an emotion, but a holy way of life.

Everyone planning to marry should approach this most pivotal life decision seriously, asking God's help and direction, listening to the thoughts and advice of their family, and honoring the counsel of mature spiritual advisers. If we take the teaching of the Gospel seriously divorce and its consequences will become rarer and rarer in our parishes and our families. ■

The Occult

During the past decades Halloween has become a major holiday, with house decorations, "Halloween lights," costumes, increasing to the point that many houses are decorated more ornately for Halloween than for Christmas. This is not surprising, because for those conscious of the spiritual and pseudo-spiritual signs of our times we see that the occult has made definite and deep inroads into our societal psyche. An occult consciousness requires an occult holiday—hence the popularity of Halloween. What are the signs of this occult consciousness in our society?

The most characteristic aspect of occult phenomena in our daily lives is that they are inherently religious practices—that is, they are based on faith—which are supposedly divested of their religious meaning. We see, for example, "psychics" on TV or in storefronts on the streets; astrology columns as a fixture of newspapers and magazines; yoga or meditation taught for "relaxation;" the strong hold of superstition upon people who live in a "scientific" culture (is there a thirteenth floor in your apartment building or workplace?); educated professionals with scientific degrees consulting witches or magicians to help solve their problems (I am not making this up); and the general rise of what is loosely termed "neo-paganism," i.e., turning one's back on God the Creator and worshiping God's creation, whether this be worship of the earth, the stars, materialistic idolatry, or self-worship.

"Whoever consults a false prophet on any matter is an idolater. Such a man is completely lacking in truth; he is foolish" (Shepherd of Hermes).

"No one shall be found among you who practices divination, or is a soothsayer, or an augur, or a sorcerer, or one who casts spells, or who consults ghosts or spirits, or who seeks oracles from the dead. For whoever does these things is abhorrent to the Lord your God" (Deut. 18:10-12).

As we see from these two quotes, the practice of "fortune-telling" is nothing new. We often have a tendency to laugh at any mention of "psychics," fortune tellers, and alike, but we should not. This is big business, with people renting storefronts in expensive neighborhoods, advertising in the yellow pages, and frequent television and radio programs dealing with such things. (In the mid-90's I remember seeing an advertisement on TV for telephone consultations with "psychics" for $4.99 a minute and wondering what would happen if I asked for $4.99 a minute to serve a baptism or wedding? You think services are long now?.)

It is important to point out that throughout history both religious and secular literature indicates that there have always been people who possess "psychic" gifts—both the bible and the lives of the saints give us many clear examples. The essential question, then, is who is bestowing this gift—God or the Devil? Quite clearly, anyone who is not of the Church, not to mention anyone who is doing this for money, is not acting on God's behalf (and it bears repeating that priests are forbidden to set "fees" for the sacraments, because *You received without paying, give without pay"* (Matt. 10:8). The devil, as we know, can perform miracles—but only by imitating God's miracles. So we must be very careful whenever anyone displays extraordinary, "paranormal" abilities, for we are warned in Holy Scripture to "test the spirits," because the devil can even appear as an "angel of light."

Consequently there are two very good reasons to avoid anything to do with any type of "fortune-telling;" first of all, we may be dealing with someone who is under diabolical delusion or even possession. The story of King Saul and the witch of En-dor (cf.1 Sam. 28) gives us the clear message that our hope should be in God, and only in God. Secondly, the "psychic" may simply be a charlatan, interested only in separating a fool from his or her money. If we do have enough "disposable income" that we wish to receive good fortune by squandering it, we are taught very clearly that it would be better for us (and for the world) were we to "squander" it by feeding the poor, giving it to a needy parish or monastery so they might pray for us, or simply donating it to the Church or some other Christian charity in order that the Gospel might be made manifest in the world. This action brings a blessing—the other a curse.

The lack of concern certain parents have for such matters was brought home to me in full force a couple of years ago when a particular Ukrainian youth organization hired one of these "psychics" to provide "entertainment" for one of their events. There were mothers not only financially supporting such foolishness, but exposing their children to it as well. When my wife found out what was going on and questioned the organizers the response was an apathetic "Oh, do you have a problem with this? What's wrong? It's just for fun." And this from people who consider themselves good Christians!

A final warning is that we need not look even to "psychics" to find such spiritual danger—it is as close as our local toy store. We have all seen so called "ouija" boards in the toy sections of department stores. This might lead us to believe that they are harmless fun. This, unfortunately, is not true. These "games" were very popular at the end of the 19th century, when "spiritism" was in vogue. They were so popular that the government wished to "get in on the action" and tax them. If they were classified as a religious item they would be exempt from taxes. But then someone realized that if they were classified as a game they could be taxed, and *voilà!*, the ouija board got a place on the shelf next to Monopoly. The ouija board is nothing more than a means for contacting disincarnate spirits—something which is forbidden to Christians. If it were necessary, or desirable for our spiritual growth, God would have made it known to us through His Holy Revelation. Since He has not, and based on the experiences of those who have in fact encountered demons through agency of the ouija board, we can say very clearly that the spirits encountered in such "harmless fun," just as those encountered through "mediums," are nothing other than fallen spirits, or demons.

In addition to the so-called "psychics," astrology is another occult practice with an enormous scope and influence. Astrology is regarded as one of the pillars of the so-called "new age" movement. The very foundation of astrology is blatantly un-Christian. Astrology teaches that the stars, constellations and planets control our actions. This is a pre-Christian pagan belief, which is obviously at odds with the Christian understanding of free will. How can the stars control my actions if I am in control of my actions?

This occult discipline was well known to the apostolic fathers. In the *Didache*, a first century Christian document, we read *"Do not foretell the future from natural signs, for this leads to idolatry. Do not use magic formulae, or study astrology or purification charms; you should not even wish to observe such things, for they all lead to idolatry."* The life of St. Cyprian (Oct. 2/15), who was a pagan priest and sorcerer before his conversion to Christianity, is a lesson in the seriousness of the matter of astrology for Christians. St. Cyprian went through the entire apprenticeship of the sorcerer, learning all the spells, incantations, how to contact demons, and the culmination of his education was the study of astrology.

Unfortunately this particular occult practice is extremely commonplace. Astrological columns are found in newspapers, magazines, variety stores, TV, radio, all around us. It is especially prevalent among our brothers and sisters from the former soviet bloc countries, as can be confirmed by a quick perusal of virtually any periodical aimed at immigrants from Eastern Europe. There is generally little mention of the Church in such periodicals unless there is a scandal involved, there is often no mention of Christ, Christian spirituality, and so forth, but one can often find at least a full page of detailed astrological forecasts in most issues.

Should Christians have anything at all to do with astrology? Obviously not. So why then do many people who call themselves Christians read about or even engage in such practices? The answer is basically the same for all of the above cited occult disciplines—out of "recreation," out of ignorance, or out of despair.

The young women who go to the psychic to get their "fortune told," like the person who sets their personal schedule according to their horoscope, might think they are simply engaging in harmless recreation, but they are in fact opening themselves up to the influence of the devil. Even though we usually conceive of the devil as an ugly being, it is important to emphasize that the appearance of the devil in our lives is just the opposite—he appears as something good and desirable. He is "the tempter," he operates not only through fear, but also through seduction. Many people engage in astrology, fortune telling or eastern mysticism through ignorance. But if a person arrives in New York from Siberia and does not know that it is dangerous to cross the street against a red light yet proceeds to do so they will quite likely suffer for their ignorance. Playing with spiritual fire simply through ignorance can be no less disastrous.

The person who is despairing, however, requires a special approach. There are those in our communities who, for example, have a difficult time dealing with the death of a loved one, the loss of a job, sickness in the family, or just plain clinical depression. It often happens that such people do not find a sympathetic ear, or a helping hand among their family, friends, or parish community. It is especially important for the Christian community, the parish, to embrace and support such people so that they do not feel the need to turn to charlatans and false prophets to receive comfort. For in this case the sin might not be personal, but rather communal.

In conclusion three points must be emphasized. First, no Christian should have anything to do with these, or other, non-Christian "spiritual" practices. Second, if we have consulted "psychics" or taken part in any other type of occult activity we should approach for confession at the first opportunity to ask God's forgiveness of this great sin, and His help in repenting. Third, the most important point to remember is that everything spiritual or supernatural which is good and holy and necessary for our salvation is found in the Church. If we are truly living the life of the Orthodox Christian there will be no need to find our solace, recreation, comfort or peace outside of the Church. ■

Cremation

The incineration of bodily remains has never been recommended or practiced by Christians. The Church has always regarded the body as holy and worthy of great respect. More and more often, though, Orthodox priests and bishops in the new world are being asked to serve funerals for church members whose remains have been or will be cremated. This request tends to cause very difficult emotional and pastoral situations whenever it is made. The family, who is already distraught at the loss of a loved one, must deal with the fact that no funeral service may be served, and may misunderstand this as the Church (or the priest, or the Bishop) "judging" the deceased.

Generally speaking, priests may only serve a funeral for a person who is to be cremated with the blessing of the local Bishop, and usually this service, if it is permitted at all, is no more than a simple Litia or trisagion for the dead. The full funeral is usually not served.

Why do people, even knowledgeable Orthodox Christians, choose to have their body cremated after death? Often we hear that "there is not enough land—if everyone will be buried we will run out of space." This is one of those arguments which seems to make sense, but it does not. If we only take for example the Orthodox countries of Greece or Bulgaria, we see that these countries, which are populated much more densely and are very much smaller than countries like the U.S.A. or Canada do not have this problem—even though they have been inhabited for thousands of years.

We hear the financial argument that "funerals cost too much; it is cheaper to cremate." Again, this generalization is not necessarily true. Yes, it is possible to spend less on a cremation, but it is possible to spend very much more also. Do not believe me, go down to your local funeral home and ask. In the end, the real reason people incinerate their bodies is simply because they want to.

What has the Orthodox Church always expected of the faithful, regarding the death and burial of her members? First of all, that anyone who is in any danger of dying will ask the priest to confess and commune them, and to serve the Mystery of the Oil (anointing of the sick). This should happen when the one who is ill is still able to speak and act for himself. Secondly, death is understood as the temporary separation of the soul from the body, and as we care for the soul through our prayers, we physically care for the body—the physical remains. After death, the body should be washed, dressed, and visited (either in the funeral home, the church or even the family home); the funeral should be served; and the body buried in the earth (as our Lord's body was) to await the General Resurrection. Thirdly, embalming, costly caskets, concrete sarcophagi (vaults), elaborate flower arrangements, limousines, and other contemporary customs are understood as being unnecessary by the Church—acceptable for those who can afford them, but definitely unacceptable if this will impose financial hardship on the family, and especially if they, not God, become the center of attention of the funeral. For many Orthodox people one of the most important parts of the funeral is the meal afterwards. Originally this was a meal where all the poor were invited to eat (and is still referred to as the "mercy meal" in some cultures), a type of charity on behalf of the deceased. The meal was traditionally of a lenten character—and if a funeral takes place on a fasting day the meal should always be lenten. There is no reason not to have a lenten meal on a fasting day here in North America, where all kinds of food is easily available.

Part of the problem regarding cremation has to do with the simple fact that the Orthodox Church has not made a definitive statement on the practice of cremation. A quick perusal of the Rudder—the compilation of the Holy Canons of the Orthodox Church—will show that there is no mention of cremation. Why, then, is cremation forbidden?

To offer what at first glance might seem to be an overly simplistic response, we might say that cremation is forbidden by the Church because it has never been practiced by the Church. You do not need to make a rule against doing something you do not do. Cremation is alien to the ethos, practice, and theological teaching of Orthodoxy. Consequently, by not practicing cremation we are adhering to the discipline of the Church—we are confessing our Orthodoxy. If the answer to the question of why people are cremated is "because they wish to be," our answer to the question of why Orthodox are not cremated is simply "because we are Orthodox!" As we say in the Creed, we believe in the Church. Following the discipline of the Church is a statement of our faith.

The Western denominations did not practice cremation until very recently (in fact, it was illegal to burn bodily remains in the British Empire until the end of the 19th century). Cremation could only gain a foothold in the "Christian" world when and where the true Christian understanding of the body was lost and a pagan (whether religious or materialistic) world-view had replaced it. We see the results of this world-view in our country and in our Churches.

As Orthodox, we should look at everything in the context of our salvation. Will cremation contribute to my salvation? Will it bring me closer to God and His Church? Is there anything essentially good, or necessary, or noble in cremation? I think that all of us can agree that the answer to all these questions is no—and that in fact the opposite may be true. And if this is in fact the case, then all of us should do our best to see that our faithful recognize that the Orthodox practice is the original and only truly Christian practice befitting all members of the Church; that our bodily remains are treated with respect and dignity after our death; and that all our faithful receive the beautiful and meaningful Orthodox funeral which is the crown of a truly Christian life. ∎

Limits and Expectations

Anyone who has friends or relatives in a former Soviet republic, or has traveled in a third world country, knows how lucky we are in Canada. It is heaven on earth. We have freedom, peace, opportunity, prosperity, abundant food and energy, you name it. So why do we have such problems as crime, violence, poverty, *et cetera*?

A number of years ago I heard a native elder being interviewed on CBC radio. He was asked how the aboriginal peoples teach their children about their rights. *"In our tradition we do not teach our children about their rights, but about their responsibilities,"* he said.

In his autobiography Tom Landry, the Hall-of-fame coach of the Dallas Cowboys football team, writes: "Most successful football players not only accept rules and limitations but need them. Players are free to perform at their best only when they know what the expectations are, where the limits stand. I see this as a principle that also applies to life, a principle our society as a whole has forgotten: You cannot enjoy true freedom without limits." In order for society to function, in order for people to live fruitful lives, we all must be able to deal with limits and expectations, and to act responsibly. We need to know where the lines are drawn, what our goals are, and to be accountable for our actions.

It is evident that a disrespect for limits and a lack of expectations are present today among almost all echelons of society. Art, movies, television, literature, theology, jurisprudence, finance, and many other disciplines are full of people "pushing the envelope." The lack of a firm sense of limits and responsibility, as well as basic common sense, are evident in the actions of people like Bill Clinton and O.J. Simpson as well as in the teenage criminal and the grade school bully.

One of the defining controversies of our society is the abortion debate. Christians, as well as others—Orthodox Jews and Muslims, for instance—believe that life begins at conception. To my knowledge there is no conclusive scientific proof to the contrary. Consequently, we believe abortion to be murder, which is, quite understandably, upsetting to those who would see it as a "right." But the fundamental problem has to do with intercourse, not conception. The lines of the abortion debate are drawn not between "pro-lifers" and "pro-choicers," but between those who desire to be irresponsible in their sexual activity (and every "unwanted" pregnancy can be defined as an irresponsible sexual encounter) and those who preach sexual responsibility.

The expectation for the Christian is monogamous sex within a stable marriage. The limit is no sex outside of marriage. The responsibility encompasses the man's sticking around and being a good husband and father, as well as the mother doing that which only a mother can do. Without limits, and without expectations, without responsibility, no one can grow up to see the wisdom and the benefit of qualities such as consideration and courtesy to all; respect for elders and those in authority; generosity and love towards the poor and the marginalized, which seem to be so lacking in our contemporary world.

We often hear that the problem is in the schools. Hogwash. Schools can help, but they can only do what is within their capabilities. The fact of the matter is that the primary responsibility for inculcating the concept of limits and expectations into our youth, and therefore into society, lies with parents. If people were to be paid according to the importance of their work it would not be athletes, entertainers and executives making the big bucks. The mothers and fathers who raise decent, hard-working, courteous, helpful, humble and respectful children are worth far more than the highest paid athlete or entertainer. And I will bet that every one of these children is raised with limits, expectations, and responsibility.

There is a tradition in our society, that when we celebrate the new year we make resolutions which we expect will improve our lives. We could not, as a society, make a better resolution than to bring respect for limits, wise and positive expectations, and a firm sense of responsibility back into fashion, and to expect nothing less from our children, our politicians, our athletes, our entertainers, and ourselves. ■

Homosexuality and Marriage

Canadian society is clearly split over the issue of homosexual marriage. Parliament, political parties, citizens and even churches are plainly and painfully divided by this question. Will changing the definition of marriage to include homosexual unions contribute to a more humane, just, and good society as some claim, or simply make an already bad situation worse?

Many arguments have been offered against the acceptance of legal marriage for homosexuals; the "natural order" argument, which assumes homosexuality is unnatural because it is incompatible with procreation; the linguistic or semantic argument, which states that the word marriage has universally been understood to refer to a relationship between people of the opposite sex; and the various arguments based on religious or moral principles.

Before going any further I should "state my bias." I am an Orthodox Christian priest. We Orthodox see ourselves as the direct descendants of the apostolic Church founded by Jesus Christ. We see our faith as simple Christianity. Our Church tradition includes almost 2,000 years of well-documented human experience, examples of saintliness, sinfulness, and everything in between. It is this faith and tradition as well as my vocation as a priest, which includes personal pastoral experience with homosexuals as well as heterosexuals that is my springboard into this discussion.

Sexual activity among people of the same gender has always been regarded by Christians as sinful. Any opinion to the contrary is simply not representative of the historical teaching of Christianity. The scriptural and historical sources are very clear, both in the Old and New Testaments. You might not agree with this opinion, you might think that those who hold such a belief are crazy, misguided, or worse, but saying "it is not so" is simply not factual.

The "Jesus never said anything against homosexuality" argument which I have read in the press is nonsense. Jesus never said "thou shalt not sexually molest young children" either. But when the scandals within the Catholic Church began to surface regarding pedophilia no one dared propose this argument. It amazes me that people who would have quite correctly excoriated the Roman Church had it tried to use this defense could turn around and use the same argument on behalf of homosexuality. It just does not fly.

The Epistles of St. Paul, as well as the Old Testament texts in which teachings about homosexuality appear pre-date the composition of the Gospels. Had there been anything "anti-Gospel" in them they would not have been accepted into the canon of Christian scripture, and there were in fact many books which were not.

On the basis of the Bible, as well as the entire tradition of the Church, the Christian understanding of homosexuality would prevent its acceptance as a blessed and potentially holy lifestyle. As far as homosexual marriage is concerned the question is quite simple: Why would the Church bless acts which it regards as sinful and unnatural?

Having said this, it is important to present a complete picture of the Christian understanding of sexual morality. St. Paul writes thus to the Corinthians: *"Neither fornicators, nor idolaters, nor adulterers, nor homosexuals, nor sodomites, nor thieves, nor covetous, nor drunkards, nor revilers, nor extortioners will inherit the kingdom of God"* (1 Cor. 9-10).

The teaching of the Church is consistent and unequivocal. Any sexual activity outside of marriage is sinful, whether homosexual or heterosexual. Consequently we see that a practicing homosexual is certainly no better than someone involved in a "common-law" marriage, or an adulterer, but they are certainly no worse.

Every age and culture has core issues—beliefs which impact upon the fundamental self-understanding and self-realization of the given culture or era. One of the core issues, if not the core issue of 21st century Canadian society (and contemporary Western society in general) is sex.

Perhaps one of the reasons acceptance of homosexuality has become so widespread is that those who wish to be sexually promiscuous have no logical grounds to forbid sexual "liberation" to anyone. And if sex really is the "big ticket item" of our society, if we live for sex, or identify ourselves and others not by race, national origin, religion, or personhood but by sexual orientation (a truly contemporary innovation), then we can only expect increased incidences of adultery, rape, fornication, unwanted children, homosexuality, bestiality, broken families, abortion and divorce as the consequence.

What is the relationship between sex and gender? Christians understand gender—maleness and femaleness—as the reflection of a divinely created order. *"And God said, 'Let us make man in Our image, after Our likeness. . . .' So God created man in His own image, in the image of God created He him; male and female created He them"* (Gen. 1:26-27).

Our gender, our maleness and femaleness, is an image of God, Who Christians believe to be a Trinity of three persons—Father, Son, and Holy Spirit. Not three Gods, but three unique and complementary persons in one God.

We do not believe that men and women are interchangeable, but rather complementary. We believe that the fullness of humanity is not found only in women, nor in men alone, but in the union of both. For Christians homosexuality is unnatural first and foremost in a theological sense, and only then in a physical sense. Homosexuality is a denial of true humanity because it does not reflect the essence of God, Who is composed of Three Persons, all different, all of Whom complement each other, none of Whom is simply "interchangeable" with another.

But do Christians, or anyone else (including atheists and homosexuals) have the right to force their particular moral code on others? C.S.Lewis in the book <u>Mere Christianity</u> states that *"There ought to be two distinct kinds of marriage: one governed by the State with rules enforced on all citizens, the other governed by the Church with rules enforced by her on her own members."* The government, citing the authority of this influential Christian writer, might say "this is exactly what we are proposing." So why don't those crazy Christian zealots stop right now, keep their beliefs within the walls of their homes and Churches, and leave the rest of us alone? Christians live in particular societies, and because they love their country and countrymen, they feel a responsibility to strive for that which will be good and beneficial for those around them.

Several years ago, when "common law" marriage was legalized, the opponents claimed that this would lead to the legal recognition of homosexual unions. At the time such statements were called "exaggeration" or "hyperbole" and dismissed. Now that this has in fact happened, what is next?

If the government can redefine the word marriage to mean simply "two people" what is to prevent them from re-defining it as a union among more than two people? If homosexuality is "natural," what is there to prevent pedophiles, as well as others with "unique" sexual preferences, from arguing that their particular lusts are "natural," and thereby claim protection under the law, claim their "right" to sexual gratification?

If I decide to ignore the law which says I must stop at a red light I will eventually cause myself and others much harm. If I decide to ignore the laws of nature—by trying to jump over Lake Ontario, or grow field tomatoes in the middle of winter, for example—I will just frustrate myself and make the people around me crazy (at best!). Divine law is no different. How much harm has been done over the last several decades by trying to separate sex from marriage, from the family, from responsibility? Nothing, especially our sexual behavior, is a strictly personal matter. The consequences of every sin, no matter how small, extend to the ends of the universe.

Human society has never known marriage between people of the same sex. Democracy was given us by the ancient Greeks—who themselves possessed a lively homosexual sub-culture. But neither they, nor any other society has institutionalized homosexual marriage before our time. Why?

People are not any more intelligent today than they were a hundred, or a thousand years ago. People today act in the same "culturally conditioned" ways they did 2,000 years ago—only the conditioning is different. During the entire course of human history no one has come up with a better way for children to be born and raised, for spouses to be psychologically and emotionally fulfilled, for society and nation to be strong, than through healthy, heterosexual, monogamous marriage. You would almost think someone planned it that way. ■

For Life

"Any country that accepts abortion is not teaching its people to love, but to use violence to get what they want. . . . the greatest destroyer of peace today is abortion, because it is a war against the child, a direct killing of the innocent child. . . . The so-called right to abortion has pitted mothers against their children and women against men. It has sown violence and discord at the heart of the most intimate human relationships. It has portrayed the greatest of gifts -a child- as a competitor, an intrusion and an inconvenience" (Mother Theresa of Calcutta).

Abortion is undoubtedly the most important and contentious issue facing western society today. The key question regarding abortion has to do with whether the aborted embryo or fetus is a living human being or not. When does life begin? Christians (like most humans throughout history) have always believed that life begins at conception, so if an embryo or fetus is a human being abortion equals murder. One of the reasons that the abortion question is so hotly debated is that it truly is a "life and death" issue.

Abortion advocates can roughly be divided into three groups regarding the question of when life begins. One group ignores the question, claiming that anything in the uterus is part of a woman's body, and base their support of abortion on the alleged right of a woman to do what she wants with her body. The second group argues that life does not begin at conception, but at a later time (e.g. the implantation of the fertilized ovum in the uterus; quickening— i.e., when the child becomes active in the womb— or physical birth). The third group claims that it does not matter when life begins, as we have the right to kill babies inside or even outside the womb.

On the basis of science and universal human experience we can state that none of these positions accords either with Christian teaching or logic. Without going into detail, and notwithstanding the miraculous and complicated nature of conception and pregnancy, we can simply ask the question "if life does not begin at conception, then when <u>does</u> it begin?" Life obviously cannot begin before conception, and there is no particular point after conception which can undeniably be acknowledged as the beginning of life.

The fact that we live in a culture which has an unhealthy understanding of freedom complicates this issue as well. Many people consider "freedom" to mean unbounded personal autonomy, a lack of any restrictions on personal conduct. One unhealthy manifestation of this distorted idea of freedom is the sexual licentiousness which is ubiquitous in our society.

Logically, the main biological purpose of sexual intercourse is procreation. The pleasure associated with sexual intercourse is God's way of encouraging us to "multiply and fill the earth." Since a human child requires decades of care in order to mature, the "unitive" aspect of human sexual intercourse—i.e., the fact that males and females who engage in sexual intercourse will under normal circumstances develop feelings of emotional attachment to each other—supports the relationship between the parents so that a child might have the benefit and support of two loving parents throughout their life.

It is not coincidental that the demand for "abortion rights" appears concurrently with the "sexual revolution" of the 60's. There is no sure fire method of birth control; sexual intercourse will sooner or later result in pregnancy. In order for women to engage in promiscuous sexual activity without the "inconvenience" of pregnancy abortion became a necessity.

The "problem" of access to abortion was "solved" in Canada in 1969 with the passage of the Liberal government's Omnibus Bill that greatly weakened Canadian abortion laws. This law, in turn, was struck down totally in 1988 by the Supreme Court, resulting in full legal abortion on demand through all nine months of pregnancy. As a result Canada is unique in the Western world in having no legal restrictions on abortion.

According to Statistics Canada approximately 110,000 children are aborted in Canada each year—i.e, about 1/3 of Canadian pregnancies end in abortion. Since 1969 over 3,000,000 children have been killed by surgical abortions and an untold number by chemical abortions. As I write these words 51 Canadian soldiers have been killed in Afghanistan over the past 5 years. Imagine if 2,115 soldiers were being killed weekly. We would rightly be concerned about the effects this would have on the demographics and the psyche of our nation.

Annual "Marches for Life" are held both in Canada and in the USA. Canadians demonstrate their opposition to abortion in Ottawa with various events during the month of May, similar to the annual event held in Washington D.C. every January. These events are interdenominational gatherings for the tens of millions of Canadians and Americans who oppose abortion and wish to make their views and presence known and felt in the nations capitals.

By participating in the March for Life or organizing similar events on a local or parochial level; lobbying our provincial, state and federal representatives to legislate against abortion; supporting shelters and programs for pregnant women so that they might truly have a "choice"—the choice to bear their child; by extending the forgiveness of Christ to those who procure or perform abortions; and by teaching our children that life is a priceless gift as well as instilling in them a healthy and holy vision of human sexuality let us do all we can to make abortion a problem of the past. ■

Slavery

She left at dusk. She kissed her parents, knowing that she would probably never see them again. She traveled mostly by night, never being sure where she would sleep or what she would eat. If caught she would be sent back—quite probably to torture or even death. After months of traveling, suffering from cold, anxiety, hunger and fatigue, she reached her goal. A new land called Canada, where she would be free to start a new life, where she would not have to live in fear because of her heritage, where she could live in peace.

This story could describe the experience of many of our post World War II "displaced persons" from Eastern Europe, but it does not. It describes the experience of thousands of Black American slaves who fled the plantations of the southern U.S. in the 19th century in order to live a life of freedom in Canada.

2007 is the two-hundredth anniversary of the abolition of the slave trade in the British Empire. February is Black History Month. This month our Afro-Canadian brothers and sisters will be reflecting upon their history and experience, thanking God for the gift of freedom, and celebrating their cultural heritage. People of any nation which have experienced the vagaries of antagonistic imperialism and statelessness can easily relate to their experience and thank God with them that the institution of slavery has been abolished.

But has it?

One of the greatest human rights abuses of our day is human trafficking. Between 600,000 and 800,000 people are trafficked annually for sexual exploitation, prostitution, or labor, with a cumulative worldwide total estimated to be in the tens of millions. The facts regarding human trafficking are frightening. It is often the most vulnerable of young people—orphans—who are recruited, then exploited. Threats, coercion, physical violence, and various forms of abuse are the stock-in-trade of those engaged in human trafficking. It is very difficult for women who are forcibly required to work in the sex-trade industry—especially those who are trafficked across borders—to escape. For those who are able to escape from their "employers," however, the stigma attached to prostitution, coupled with the lack of awareness and supportive legislation in most countries often conspire to place them in an even more difficult situation than the one they fled.

It is estimated that 15,000 young women from Ukraine alone are currently being exploited within the sex-trade industry in Canada.

What can be done to combat this multi-national, billion dollar "industry?" The solution consists of protection, prosecution, and prevention.

After a person has been lured from their home under false pretenses, illegally smuggled across international borders, had their passport confiscated by their "owner," forced to work in the most degrading and deplorable conditions, and abused mentally, physically and verbally, they are in a very precarious state. They need to feel safe, protected, and respected. Often, though, they are treated as criminals. As Canadians or Americans it is extremely important that we do everything possible to ensure that a legal, social and medical infrastructure is in place to help them recover from their trauma and return, as much as possible, to normal life.

The role of government is obviously important in this process, but the role of Churches and civic organizations is not to be underestimated. The sad fact is that former Soviet bloc and predominantly Orthodox countries like Ukraine, Romania, Russia, Bulgaria, and others, are the countries of origin for a disproportionately large number of trafficked women. Who better than Ukrainians to help Ukrainian victims of human trafficking, or Romanians to help Romanians, and so forth?

Prosecution of those who engage in this modern day slave trade is an important means of trying to control and diminish this problem. The laws of most countries, however, have not kept pace with the realities of human trafficking. A successful strategy for prosecution requires that the laws and resources necessary to prosecute offenders are coupled with the programs and resources necessary to help women escape this condition.

Prevention consists of increasing public awareness about the reality of human trafficking. We might begin by reading Victor Malarek's disturbing book <u>The Natashas</u>, or promote and take part in the various forums and programs organized in Canada or the U.S.A. to educate ourselves and others about this issue. In addition, we might support programs in places like Eastern Europe which teach young people how the traffickers operate and forewarn them against the offer which sounds too good to be true—and is. Prevention also consists of raising the economic standard of poorer countries like those of Eastern Europe and Southeast Asia so that the desperation which pushes people into making tragic decisions can be eliminated.

In 1807 the British Parliament abolished the slave trade. In 1863 Abraham Lincoln signed the Emancipation Proclamation. Grateful to God, we celebrate these accomplishments with our Afro-Canadian and Afro-American brothers and sisters.

But in 2007 human slavery still exists.

Let us all do what we can to fight the evil of human trafficking. Each of us alone can do little. But together, with the cooperative efforts of our churches, organizations, and governmental agencies, we can achieve much towards ending this hideous practice, saving the souls and the lives of its victims. ■